All Generations Will Call Me Blessed

৯৯

My soul magnifies the Lord,
and my spirit rejoices in God my Savior,
for he has looked with favor on the lowliness
of his servant.
Surely, from now on
all generations will call me blessed;
for the Mighty One has done great things for me,
and holy is his name.

—Luke 1:47–49

All Generations Will Call Me Blessed

MARY AT THE MILLENNIUM

JIM MCMANUS, C.SS.R.

A Crossroad Book
The Crossroad Publishing Company
New York

12\99

The Crossroad Publishing Company
370 Lexington Avenue, New York, NY 10017

Printed in the United States of America

Scripture quotations are from *The New Jerusalem Bible,* published by Darton
Longman & Todd. All quotations from the documents of the Second Vatican
Council are from the 1996 edition of *Constitutions, Decrees, and Declarations,*
edited by Austin Flannery, O.P., published by Dominican Publications, Dublin,
Ireland, and are quoted with permission. The author and publisher wish to
thank SCM Press, London, for permission to quote from Jacques Bur, *How to
Understand the Virgin Mary.*

Library of Congress Cataloging-in-Publication Data

McManus, Jim, 1938–
    All generations will call me blessed : Mary at the millennium /
Jim McManus
      p. cm.
    Includes bibliographical references.
    ISBN 0-8245-1787-3 (pbk.)
    1. Mary, Blessed Virgin, Saint. 2. Catholic Church—Doctrines.
I. Title.
BT602.M385   1999
232.91–dc21   99-22092
                                      CIP

1   2   3   4   5   6   7   8   9   10   03   02   01   00   99

232.91
MCM

In Memory of Damien

Contents

Introduction

WHEN I RECEIVED THE INVITATION to write this book on Our Lady, my first reaction was one of apprehension. I am not a mariologist, that is, I have never specialized in the theology of Mary's role in the mystery of Christ and the church. I was not qualified for the task. Then I found myself saying, "but Mary is someone whom I have known and loved all my life." I knew at once that I should gratefully accept the invitation and write this book.

As I began to think and pray about the task that I had taken on, the plan for the book evolved. Mary was at the center of the good news of Jesus Christ, which I preached on parish missions and retreats. I would approach the writing of the book in the same spirit. My objective would be to tell others what I know about Mary, how I came to know and love her, and how and why we should be devoted to her. This objective clarified my method. I would first of all look at the sources of revelation, the Scriptures, and see what the word of God tells us about Mary the Mother of God; I would then find out what the Christians in the first five centuries of the church, when there were no such divisions as Catholic and Protestant, thought about Mary. Then I would reflect on what the church has taught throughout the ages and is teaching today about Mary. This scriptural, historical, and theological reflection would constitute the first half of the book. The second half of the book would look at the consequences of Catholic doctrine on Mary in terms of devotion. I would consider what devotion to Mary is, how it is expressed in the public worship of the church and in private and personal prayer. Finally I would conclude with a reflection on how Mary's spirituality is relevant for us in the third millennium.

I want to write about Mary primarily from the word of God. What does God say to us about the woman we know as Mary? The Second Vatican Council, in a wonderful passage in the Dogmatic Constitution on Divine Revelation, says:

> In the sacred books the Father who is in heaven comes lovingly to meet his children and talks with them. And such is the force and the power of the word of God that it is the church's support and strength, imparting robustness to the faith of its daughters and sons and providing food for their souls. It is a pure and unfailing fount of spiritual life. (*Dei Verbum* 21)

In the Scriptures we encounter many different cultures and languages; we can explore different periods of human history; we hear many different human voices. But what makes the Scriptures the word of God is the fact that God the Father comes "lovingly to meet" and talk with us. We will try to allow the Father to meet us in the Scriptures about Mary; we will try to learn from how previous generations in the church understood Mary and fulfilled her prophecy by calling her blessed.

St. Alphonsus de Liguori, the founder of my religious family, the Redemptorists, insisted that his brothers should preach on Mary on all missions and retreats. He knew from his own experience the truth of what the Vatican Council would say in the Dogmatic Constitution on the Church: "Having entered deeply into the history of salvation, Mary, in a way, unites in her person and re-echoes the most important doctrines of the faith; and when she is the subject of preaching and veneration she prompts the faithful to come to her Son, to his sacrifice, to the love of the Father" (*Lumen Gentium* 65). Preaching about Mary the Mother of Jesus always encourages a deeper conversion of heart. We preach or talk or write about Mary not because we want to bring people to her but because we want to make Jesus Christ her Son known. My esteemed professor and confrere Fr. Bernard Häring, in response to my question about his own devotion to Mary, wrote as follows just a few months before he died: "How could I love Jesus without loving Him together with his Mother? How could I not love Mary with the very love of Jesus? My devotion to Mary was always a devotion of heart and expressed itself frequently, regularly and spontaneously." Another great theologian of our times, Karl Rahner, when asked why there was a decline in devotion to Mary, famously responded that modern theology has gone in for abstractions and abstractions don't need a mother!

In writing this book I had the support of many people, especially my community in London. Often, when I was stalled in writing, a confrere's encouraging inquiry—"How's the book on Mary coming on?"—got me started again. I am grateful to them. I owe a special word of thanks to my confrere Richard Reid, who read the manuscript and made some very helpful suggestions. Two friends, an Anglican priest in England and a Presbyterian minister in Scotland, responded to my request for their personal contribution to this book. I wish to thank them. Finally, I am grateful to Lynn Schmitt Quinn, my editor, who asked me to write this book on Mary at the Millennium.

Mary: The First
and Perfect Disciple

ACH MORNING I SAY A PRAYER to Our Lady that begins with the words "Most holy Virgin Mary, perfect disciple of Jesus Christ . . . ." I didn't always address Mary as a "disciple of Jesus." I honored her as his mother. It never occurred to me even to ask the question whether or not she was also his disciple. I was, therefore, quite shocked when I first came across writings that seemed to indicate that Mary never became a disciple during the Lord's public ministry. Rosemary Radford Ruether, for example, wrote, "The mother does not seem to be a follower during Jesus' lifetime. She is even hostile to his mission."[1]

My Catholic sense of piety was outraged by the view that Mary might have been hostile to the mission of Jesus. Did the Gospels express any reservations about Mary's faith in and support for her son's mission? In the view of the authors of the rightly acclaimed ecumenical study *Mary in the New Testament,* "No NT verse ever says specifically that Jesus' mother did not believe in him."[2]

Once such a question has been asked, however, it has to be answered. I found the answer given very clearly in a sermon that St. Augustine preached over fifteen hundred years ago. Augustine says:

> I beg you to listen to what the Lord had to say when he stretched out his hand towards his disciples: "Here are my mother and my brethren" and "whoever does the will of my Father in heaven is my brother and sister and my mother." Are

we to take it from this that the Virgin Mary did not do the will of the Father, she who by faith believed, by faith conceived; she who was chosen to bring forth salvation among men: by Christ created that Christ in her might be created? Indeed and indeed she did the Father's will and it is a greater thing for her that she was Christ's disciple than that she was his mother. It is a happier thing to be his disciple than to be his mother. (Office of Readings for Feast of Presentation)

This clear teaching of St. Augustine has been restated in our own time by Pope Paul VI:

First, the Virgin Mary has always been proposed to the faithful by the Church as an example to be imitated not precisely in the type of life she led, and much less for the socio-cultural background in which she lived and which today scarcely exists anywhere. She is held up as an example to the faithful rather for the way in which, in her own particular life, she fully and responsibly accepted the will of God (cf. Luke 1:38), because she heard the word of God and acted on it and because charity and a spirit of service were the driving force of her actions. She is worthy of imitation because she was the first and most perfect of Christ's disciples. (*To Honor Mary* 35)

Pope John Paul II writes in his encyclical *Redemptoris mater* (*Mother of the Redeemer*):

Thus in a certain sense Mary as Mother became the first "disciple" of her Son, the first to whom he seemed to say "Follow me," even before he addressed this call to the Apostles or to anyone else. (§22)

Discipleship

The fact that Mary was the first and perfect disciple of Jesus establishes common ground between her and us. Discipleship is what we all have in common. But what constitutes discipleship? We can identify a number of common factors:

The disciple is called personally. It is not a matter of private, personal initiative. The initiative belongs entirely to Christ. Jesus says, as he said to Peter and Andrew, "follow me and I will make you fishers of men" (Matt.

4:19). Acceptance of his invitation calls for a radical change in their lives: "And they left their nets at once and followed him" (Matt. 4:20). From being students of the art of fishing they became students of the life, the work, the teaching, the attitude, the whole personality of Jesus. As disciples they would learn not just his teaching; they would learn about how he lived, how he loved, how he reached out in compassion.

The disciple is committed. In answering the call the disciple must make life-changing decisions. Without a deep commitment to the person of Jesus, the disciple will never make these changes or persevere in the new way of life. This commitment, the fruit of grace, deepens and grows as the disciple remains faithful.

Jesus himself gave this condition for discipleship: "If you make my word your home, you will indeed be my disciples, you will learn the truth and the truth will make you free" (John 8:31). Relationship with the word of God, the word of Jesus, is central to the experience of the disciple. Disciples not only listen to the word; they make their home in the word. They immerse themselves in the word. The word of God creates their whole spiritual environment.

ৡ৯

The Scriptural Basis of Mary's Discipleship

Let's examine the scriptural basis for Pope Paul's statement that Mary "was the first and most perfect of Christ's disciples." The Gospels recognize that Mary is the Mother of Jesus, but do they also recognize that Mary is a disciple of Jesus? In the Gospels we have four different accounts, four different memories of the life and ministry of Jesus. The Gospels are not simple biographies of Jesus. The Gospels were written several decades after the death and resurrection of Jesus. Long before the Gospels of Jesus Christ were written they were preached. Christ's command was "go and preach the gospel." Through this preaching faith in Jesus Christ spread and Christian communities were established—in Jerusalem, in Antioch, in Thessalonica, in Corinth, in Ephesus, and in Rome. Wherever the disciples went they witnessed to Jesus, and men and women were converted. They learned about the life and the teaching of Jesus. They were introduced to the celebration of the Eucharist, in which the Lord himself became present to them. The formation of Christian communities through the preaching of the gospel, the celebration of the mystery of Christ in baptism and the Eucharist, and the instruction of the new converts in the faith were all well under way for at least forty years before the first Gospel was written.

The four evangelists recorded the memories of Jesus' life and mission, which were still vivid in the Christian communities in which they lived. Each Gospel emerged from a quite different Christian community. Consequently, the memories of Jesus, recorded under the guidance of the Holy Spirit, although similar, are also quite distinct. Among these memories of all that Jesus "did and taught" (Acts 1:1) were memories of Mary, the mother of Jesus. Wherever the gospel of Jesus, the Son of God born as a human being, was preached, people had to be told about his mother. Three of the Gospels—Matthew, Mark, and Luke, known as the Synoptics—frequently recount the same event, while each evangelist at the same time provides his own distinctive reflection or interpretation. We find one memory of an encounter between Mary and Jesus recorded in all three Gospels with each evangelist giving his own distinctive gloss or interpretation. At issue was Jesus' family and their relationship with him. Does the fact that they are family mean that they have automatic access to the kingdom that Jesus is preaching, or must they too enter the kingdom through faith and repentance? As family, do they automatically qualify for discipleship? The three Gospels, each in its own way, make it very clear that blood ties or family relationships in themselves give no access to the kingdom. To get the flavor of how each of the evangelists deals with this question we will place their accounts side by side (RSV):

Matthew 12:46–50	*Mark 3:31–35*	*Luke 8:19–21*
While he was still speaking to the people, behold his mother and his brothers stood out-	And his mother and brothers came; and standing outside they sent to him and called	Then his mother and brothers came to him, but they could not reach him for the

side, asking to speak to him. Someone told him, "Your mother and your brothers are standing outside asking to speak to you." But he replied to the man who told him, "Who is my mother, and who are my brothers?" And stretching out his hand toward his disciples, he said, "Here are my mother and my brothers! For whoever does the will of my Father in heaven is my brother, and sister and mother."

him. And a crowd was sitting about him; and they said to him, "Your mother and brothers are outside, asking for you." And he replied, "Who are my mother and my brothers?" And looking around at those who sat about him, he said, "Here are my mother and my brothers! Whoever does the will of God is my brother, my sister and my mother."

crowd. And he was told, "Your mother and your brothers are standing outside, desiring to see you." But he said to them, "My mother and my brothers are those who hear the word of God and do it."

૪ઽ

St. Mark

It is clear that we are dealing with the same incident in the life of Jesus. The fact that the three Gospels report the same event is in itself significant. Equally significant are the differing recollections of this event. Each evangelist reported the story to illustrate his primary theological purpose or catechetical intent. The context of the story, then, is of vital importance for a correct understanding. Mark places his story in the context of a growing controversy surrounding Jesus and his work and a corresponding growing concern on the part of his family. The family members have two distinct causes for concern. First of all, large crowds of people are thronging around Jesus and preventing him and his disciples from eating. Second, Jesus' enemies have begun a campaign of vilification. We will look at how Mark records both these stories:

> He went home again, and once more such a crowd collected that they could not even have a meal. When his relatives heard

this, they set out to take charge of him, convinced that he was
out of his mind. (Mark 3:20-21)

Some commentators argue that it was not the relatives who
were convinced that Jesus was out of his mind but that others
were saying that he was out of his mind. Other commentators
also claim that the phrase translated "out of his mind" really
refers to the crowd around Jesus. It was "out of its mind" with
enthusiasm. Whatever the correct interpretation, Jesus' relatives
felt they had to intervene. They based their right to intervene on
their family connection. He was family; he belonged to them. In
the context of his mission, Jesus will either have to yield to the
demands of his family or redefine what being "his family" means
in the kingdom of God.

Mark tells us about the campaign of vilification of Jesus:
"The scribes who had come down from Jerusalem were saying,
'Beelzebub is in him' and, 'It is through the prince of devils that
he casts devils out'" (Mark 3:22). Jesus now engages the scribes in
a long discussion, warning them about the consequences of blas-
pheming against the Holy Spirit. After this controversy with the
scribes, Jesus' family arrives. It is in this context that Jesus asks
the question, "Who are my mother and my brothers?" The context is one of mounting controversy surrounding Jesus' ministry.
The members of his family, concerned for his welfare, believe
they have a right to intervene. Jesus makes it very clear that he
understands family connections in quite a new way. Mark writes,
"And looking round at those sitting in a circle about him, he said,
'Here are my mother and my brothers. Anyone who does the will
of God, that person is my brother and sister and mother'" (Mark
3:34-35). Jesus is saying that those who listen to the word of God
are his family. He will therefore stay with his family.

The Gospel of Mark is the earliest of the Gospels. According
to the majority of scholars, it was written sometime between the
years A.D. 65 and 75.[3] Its theme is basically the call to discipleship,
with all the challenge involved—persecution, rejection by family,
loss of friends. We can only become disciples of Christ through
faith and commitment. As George Montague says, "It is a disci-

pleship of the cross."[4] Jesus' family has no advantage over anyone else. Mark sets a scene in which Jesus' disciples are gathered around him with his mother and family on the outside. Too much, however, should not be read into this text. Jesus did not deny that his mother and family were disciples. He redefined what it meant to be members of the new family that he was calling into being by the proclamation of the kingdom of God. In this new family, his mother, brothers, and sisters would be those who do the will of God. The fact that Jesus redefined the origin of family relationships in the kingdom is no reason to conclude that he was at the same time denying that his mother and his relatives enjoyed this new relationship. He is making clear that if Mary wants to be "the mother of Jesus" in the kingdom she must attain this by her faith, by her discipleship, and by her conformity to God's will. In the light of the rest of the New Testament we have no hesitation in saying that Mary is the mother of Jesus on all accounts—the flesh and blood mother and the faith mother.

Mark's account of this encounter between Jesus and his family does seem to imply some degree of aloofness or indifference to his family. Mark's intention, however, is theological and catechetical. Discipleship begins through faith and not through blood relationship. As a good teacher, Mark is contrasting two types of relationships with Jesus—the natural relationships of the human family and the faith relationships of the new family in the kingdom. "The point of the passage is to define the eschatological family, not to exclude the physical family."[5]

Mark is also emphasizing that discipleship is hard. It calls for a total commitment in faith to the person of Christ. What better visual image could he use than to describe a scene where the natural family is outside the circle, on the fringe of the crowd, and the disciples are in the inner circle listening to Jesus. The conclusion that Mark wants his reader to draw from this graphic lesson on discipleship is not that Mary and the relatives remained on the outside but that the natural bonds of family are not in themselves sufficient for discipleship. Mark is not trying to convey that Jesus had no affection or respect for his mother. Jesus upholds respect for parents: "Honor your father and your mother"; and "Anyone who curses father or mother must be put to death" (Mark 7:10). Mark is focusing on the bonds that unite people with their Savior—the bonds of discipleship, which are established through faith and conversion.

It must be admitted, however, that Mark's scene is not the favorite Catholic scene. We don't have any great works of art depicting the family of Jesus on the outside with his disciples as part of his inner circle. From the ecumenical point of view Walter Brennan's observation is pertinent:

> Mark's Gospel has been the favorite Gospel of Protestant Christians, while Matthew's Gospel was the most read in Catholic liturgies for a long time. Matthew adds to Mark. So does Luke. Our Protestant brothers and sisters should remember that. Catholics should understand that preference for Mark has influenced Protestant estimation of Mary.[6]

But even in Mark, we have to say, there are no grounds for excluding Mary from discipleship during the life of Jesus.

ℬ

St. Matthew

The fact that Matthew modified Mark's account of this encounter between Jesus and his mother indicates that there was a different memory in Matthew's community. Gone altogether is the story of Jesus' relatives thinking that he was out of his mind. Matthew's Gospel records the fact that Jesus was virginally conceived. (Mark makes no reference to the birth of Jesus.) Matthew could not but be influenced by the knowledge that Mary knew that Jesus was conceived by the power of the Holy Spirit, that his mission was "to save his people from their sins" (Matt. 1:22). Since she knew his divine origin and mission, she could hardly think that he was out of his mind when he began to fulfill that mission. Matthew, therefore, makes no reference at all to Jesus' family being opposed to his mission or thinking that he was out of his mind. In his depiction of the scene Matthew focuses on the disciples around Jesus: "stretching out his hands towards his disciples he said, "Here are my mother and brothers. Anyone who does the will of my Father in heaven is my brother and sister and mother" (Matt. 12:50). The teaching is still the same as in Mark: the family of Jesus are those who do the Father's will, his disciples. But the tone is somewhat milder. Moreover, there is not the contrast that we have in Mark of the mother and brothers on the outside and the disciples on the inside around Jesus. Bertrand Buby comments: "Matthew has prepared us for the stage of Christological and Marian development. He has spoken reverently of the mother of the Messiah. He sets the stage for Luke who will allow the virgin to speak for herself."[7]

ℰঌ

St. Luke

Luke presents the same scene of this very public encounter between Jesus and Mary and his family but in a very different context and light. All the apparent negative attitudes that we can get from Mark are absent. While Mark sets the scene of the encounter in the context of the rumors that Jesus was out of his mind and the accusations of the scribes that he was casting out evil spirits by the power of Beelzebub, Luke presents the scene in the context of the parable of the sower. In the opinion of the authors of *Mary in the New Testament,* "The Lucan context underlines the fact that the mother and brothers are examples of the fate of the seed that has fallen in good soil."[8]

In Luke's mind Mary and the family of Jesus are disciples. It could hardly be otherwise. Luke places Mary and "the brothers of the Lord" in the midst of the disciples as they were waiting and praying for the outpouring of the Spirit at the first Pentecost (Acts 1:14). Luke also devoted the first two chapters of his Gospel to

Jesus' infancy—the story of the Annunciation, the birth, the presentation in the temple and the finding in the temple. Throughout these two chapters he is telling us about Mary—about her faith, her courage, and her presence of mind when she is visited by an archangel; her alacrity in accepting God's invitation to motherhood; and her habit of pondering God's word in her heart. In these chapters Luke describes a young woman who is spiritually and emotionally very mature, who is morally very courageous, and who lives a spirituality of praise of her Maker. In Luke's mind not only is Mary a disciple; she is a model for disciples.

℘

Kecharitōmenē—Highly Favored

The first thing that Luke recalls about Mary is that God, when he sent the angel to her, didn't address her by her own name. He gave her a new name. He called her in Greek *kecharitōmenē*, a word that we have traditionally translated as "full of grace." The angel said, "Rejoice, so highly favored," or, in our traditional translation, "Hail, full of grace" (Luke 1:28). Mary is the one who has been transformed by grace. Long before God asked her to become the mother of Jesus, Mary has been transformed by grace. She can truly say with St. Paul, "Blessed be the God and Father of our Lord Jesus Christ, who has blessed us with all the spiritual blessings of heaven in Christ" (Eph. 1:3-4). The living tradition of the church tells us that this transforming power of grace was at work in Mary right from the first moment of her existence. Mary was never in "the state of sin," alienated from God through original sin or actual sin. God's grace, which transforms and makes holy, was always effective in Mary. Mary stands out as the one who depends totally on God's grace and not on her own merits. In the presence of God, from the very first moment of her conception, that is who Mary is: she is the graced one, the transformed and holy one. She is *kecharitōmenē*. "The Fathers of the Church such as Origen and Ambrose make the observation that in the entire Bible the form *kecharitōmenē* is only applied to Mary."[9] Pope John Paul writes: "He calls her thus as if it were her real name. He does not call her by her properly earthly name: Miryam (Mary), but *by this new name: "full of grace."* What does this name mean? Why does the archangel address the Virgin of Nazareth in this way?" (*Redemptoris mater* 8). In presenting Mary as the one who has been transformed by grace, Luke is showing us how God prepared her for her vocation and mission.

This new name that the angel gave her troubled Mary. We know, from Jewish tradition, that Mary would have been about twelve and a half or thirteen years of age at the time of this angelic visitation. Luke takes this opportunity to give us our first glimpse at how this young girl reacted to this strange greeting: "she was deeply disturbed by these words and asked herself what this greeting could mean" (Luke 1:30). She reflected on the meaning of the angel's words. Interestingly, while Luke tells us that Zechariah was disturbed by the sight of the angel, he says Mary was disturbed by the words of the angel. Mary is fully alert, conscious both of the meaning of the words and of how she understood herself. How could the angel's words relate to herself? She didn't see herself as one who had been transformed by grace. Then the angel, recognizing her fears and this time using her own name, said "Mary, do not be afraid: you have won God's favor. Listen! You are to conceive and bear a son, and you must name him Jesus." Mary is not disturbed by these words, but she asks for a clarification: "But how can this come about since I am a virgin?" Then the angel tells her: "The Holy Spirit will come upon you and the power of the Most High will cover you with its shadow. And so the child will be holy and will be called Son of God" (Luke 1:35). That this answer satisfies Mary is a clear sign that she was familiar with the Spirit of God and the way the Spirit of God had been at work in her people. She was totally open to the Holy Spirit and she welcomed the coming of the Spirit. She knew the promise of God, "The days are approaching when I will pour out my Spirit on all humanity" (Joel 3:1). This promise was now going to be fulfilled in her. The Holy Spirit will come upon her. Now that the angel has given his explanation on the part of God, what is Mary going to say? No one has captured the spiritual tension of this moment better than St. Bernard. He writes:

> O Virgin, you have heard the announcement of the event, you have also heard how it will come to pass. The one and the other is marvellous, the one and the other fill us with joy. Shout for joy, Daughter of Sion, rejoice heartily, O Daughter of Jerusalem (Zc 9:9); and since joy and mirth have sounded in your ears, we also would like to hear from your mouth the response of joy; we desire this so that the bones you have crushed might rejoice (Is 51:10). . . . The angel awaits your response. We, too, await, O Sovereign, the word of mercy. . . . O Virgin, give your response without delay. . . . O Virgin blessed, open your heart to fidelity, your lips for "yes," your body for the Creator. Behold, the Desire of all the nations knocks at the door (Rv 3:20). Oh, if he should go away because of your hesitation, you will leave again, full of affliction, looking for the lover of your soul (Sg 5:6). Arise, run, open! Arise with your faith, run with your devotion, open with your "yes." (Office of Readings, 20 December)

ॐ

Mary's Enthusiastic Response

St. Bernard lyrically dramatizes the spiritual significance of this moment when the angel awaits Mary's response. Not only did the explanation of how this could come about satisfy Mary, but it also filled her with a great enthusiasm for her new role and her new relationship with the Spirit of God. She said to the angel, in our traditional phrase, "Let it be done unto me according to thy word." This well-known response of Mary can be interpreted as meaning that Mary was merely passive and resigned. Far from being passively resigned, however, she was actively engaged in entering into a partnership with God. As John McHugh points out, the correct translation of "let it be done unto me" is a cry of joy, "O may it be so for me, according to thy word." McHugh notes that the verb "let it be done" is in the optative mood in Greek, which is used to express a wish or a desire.[10] And I. de la Potterie comments: "The 'fiat' (let it be done unto me) of Mary is not just a simple acceptance and even less, a resignation. It is rather a joyous desire to collaborate with what God foresees for her. It is the joy of total abandonment to the good will of God. Thus the joy of this ending responds to the invitation to joy at the beginning."[11] Having heard God's explanation of how she was to become the mother of Jesus, Mary yearned to see God's plan fulfilled. Oh yes, let the Holy Spirit come, is her answer to the angel. She was not just a passive recipient of the divine plan. She was an active, intelligent, and courageous collaborator with God. In the words of St. Paul, we were at the "appointed time," God's time, the "fullness of time," when Mary said her definitive yes to God. Paul wrote, "When the appointed time came God sent his Son, born of a woman, born under the Law, to redeem the subjects of the Law and to enable us to be adopted as Sons" (Gal. 4:4).

With this wonderful and astounding knowledge of Mary's standing as *kecharitōmenē* in the presence of God and of her active and enthusiastic consent to God's plan, Luke would have been amazed had someone asked him whether Mary was a true disciple. He would surely have agreed with Gilberte Baril's comment:

> At the very moment she accepts the maternal mission to which she is destined by God Mary thus inaugurates "Christian" faith: she is a believer for whom God's word is enough. . . . she is the first Christian disciple.[12]

Throughout the Gospel Luke presents Mary as a woman of faith, as a disciple faithfully listening to the word and pondering it in her heart. Mary, like all disciples, lived by faith, not by knowledge. We would do Mary a great disservice if we concluded that because she knew that her son was conceived by the power of the Holy Spirit she understood everything about him. Luke presents

Mary as pondering over what was being said about Jesus or what Jesus himself was saying. Right from the night of his birth this pondering begins. Speaking about the shepherds who came, in response to the angels' message, to visit the child when he was born, Luke writes, "When they saw the child they repeated what they had been told about him, and every one who heard it was astonished at what the shepherds had to say. As for Mary, she treasured all these things and pondered them in her heart" (Luke 2:19). Mary had been told by the angel at the Annunciation all that the shepherds had been told. Yet, when she hears it repeated by them, she ponders it afresh. Yes, she knows that Jesus her son was conceived by the power of God's Spirit; he is the Son of God. How could Mary grasp that? She had to accept it in faith and ponder its meaning, just as you and I have to accept in faith that we too are God's children and ponder the meaning of that.

℘

The "Sword of Discrimination"

Mary has to engage in this same contemplative act of pondering when she and Joseph bring the child to the temple to present him to the Lord. The old prophet Simeon took the child in his arms and blessed God and said, "My eyes have seen the salvation which you have prepared for all the nations to see" (Luke 2:30). This praise of her son sends Mary into her spiritual activity of pondering, and while she is pondering Simeon addresses her directly and says, "You see this child: he is destined for the fall and the rising of many in Israel, destined to be a sign that is rejected— and a sword will pierce your own soul too— so that the secret thoughts of many hearts may be laid bare" (Luke 2:34). There has been much discussion of this sword. Popular piety has seen in the sword Mary's suffering at the foot of the cross. But Luke could not have had that in mind because, in his account of the crucifixion, Mary is not numbered among those said to be present on Calvary. It is only from the Gospel according to St. John, written a few decades after Luke, that we learn that Mary was on Calvary. How are we to understand the sword today? Many authors agree that "by the imagery of the sword passing through Mary's soul, Luke describes the difficult process of learning that obedience to the word of God transcends family ties."[13] It is a "sword of discrimination." Jesus himself spoke about bringing a sword: "Do not suppose that I have come to bring peace to the earth; it is not peace I have come to bring, but a sword" (Matt. 10:37). In Luke's version of this saying he substitutes division for sword: "Do you suppose that I am here to bring peace on earth? No, I tell you, but rather division" (Luke 12:51). The sword of the Gospel, the sword of the word of God, divides hearts, causes division in households, separates even the closest relationships. Whatever is not of God will be revealed: "the secret thoughts of many will be revealed." This sword of the word pierced Mary's heart too. She was challenged. Raymond Brown writes:

> If his sword of discrimination is to divide families, that is possible even for his own family. In the fall and the rise of many in Israel Mary will stand with the lesser number who rise—she will belong to the handful of one hundred and twenty who emerge from the ministry of Jesus as a company of believers (Acts 1:12–15)— only because like the others she has passed the test and recognized the sign. And indeed her special anguish, as the sword of discrimination passes through her soul, will consist in recognizing that the claims of Jesus' heavenly Father outrank any human attachments between him and his mother, a lesson that she will begin to learn in the very next scene (Luke 2:48–50).[14]

Pondering was Mary's response too when she lost the boy Jesus. Those were anxious days for her and Joseph, and she said so to Jesus: "'My child, why have you done this to us? See how worried your father and I have been, looking for you.' 'Why were you looking for me,' he replied. 'Did you not know that I must be busy with my Father's affairs?' But they did not understand what he meant. He then went down with them and came to Nazareth and lived under their authority. His mother stored up all these things in her heart" (Luke 2:49–51). Mary didn't always understand her son. She was worried, probably very worried. But Jesus seems to have dismissed her worry: "Why were you looking for me?" What mother wouldn't look for a boy of eleven lost in a fairly large city? If Mary knew what Jesus implied —"Did you not know that I must be busy with my Father's affairs?"—she wouldn't have worried. But she didn't know that. The sword of discrimination. The Father's will and the Father's kingdom come first in her son's life. This is the purifying and painful lesson she had to learn. She would never seek to dissuade him, but she didn't always understand him. In her life and journey of faith she had to question and ponder and live without clear answers. Like her son, she too had to grow in wisdom and grace as she opened her whole life to the mystery of Jesus. In her pondering, her faith matured. In one of his Sunday homilies Pope John Paul II reflects on this:

> We must note, however, that the purpose of "memory," according to the Bible, is essentially dynamic, actualizing: it pushes ahead. And the reason is this: what God brought about in the past to help his people is a guarantee that he will act in the same way in the present circumstances and in the future (cf. Deut. 7:17–21), since his love is eternal and unchangeable (Ps. 136:1). Therefore Mary Most Holy, too, with regard to the words and deeds of Jesus, exercised an active memory. On the one hand she "preserves" the remembrance of those words and deeds; on the other, however, the intellect strives to examine them, "reflecting on them" (Luke 2:19b: Greek *symballousa*), trying to understand their proper meaning and give them an exact interpretation.[15]

Mary, the perfect disciple, teaches all disciples the art of contemplation. But if we are going to learn the art, we will have to first treasure in our hearts, in our "active memory," the words and the deeds of Christ, and the many and varied ways that God enters our life.

St. Luke, who pays so much attention to Mary in the first two chapters of the Gospel, while dealing with the infancy of

Jesus, pays surprisingly little attention to her as he recalls the public ministry of Jesus. The authors of *Mary in the New Testament* offer this explanation:

> Once we realize that such an interest was not primarily in Mary as a person but in Mary as a symbol of discipleship, Luke's shift of attention becomes more intelligible. When Jesus was an infant, the mother was really the only appropriate figure to illustrate discipleship. . . . But in the narrative of Jesus' ministry, there is a wider range of figures who can illustrate discipleship, especially the Twelve.[16]

Mary is Jesus' first disciple, the first to live by Christian faith. She is the disciple who teaches us to say a joyous yes to the will of God in our life; she teaches us how to treasure the things that have been said about Jesus in our hearts; she teaches us how to ponder God's ways. But, as Catharina Halkes writes:

> Now the unique thing about Mary is that her attitude of "hearing and doing" coincides with becoming a mother, indeed these were the conditions for that. The unfortunate thing is that her *"fiat"* is interpreted by a male church as a timid and passive reaction to an amazing word of God. But that tells us more about the interpreters. Mary freely and actively says yes as an autonomous person who in believing receptiveness is open to salvation from God and responds to that. If people want to talk about dependence, then they should recognise that here God made himself dependent on a human being, and the human being was receptive to God.[17]

The Mary of the Synoptic Gospels, despite the problems posed by Mark, is clearly a disciple, the first disciple, the woman of faith who gave her joyous consent and entered into the wonderful partnership with God to which we owe the incarnation and our salvation.

Mary the Mother
of the Disciple

M ARY APPEARS TWICE in St. John's Gospel. On both occasions Jesus speaks to her, but he doesn't call her "mother"; he calls her "woman." When she is referred to in this Gospel, she is always called "the mother of Jesus"; she is never called "Mary." On her first appearance she speaks twice; on her second appearance she remains silent. In all she speaks nine words. Were we to judge her significance by the frequency of her appearances or the number of her words, we would have to conclude that she didn't have much of a role to play in John's Gospel. Yet all our instincts tell us that this is not the case. Her significance and role cannot simply be measured by either the frequency of her appearances or the volume of her words. We are conscious of the symbolic setting in which the appearances occur. Many highly technical books and articles have been written on this subject in the past twenty years.

Signs

John doesn't speak about Jesus working miracles; rather, he tells us that Jesus worked "signs." Thus, while we can understandably talk about the miracle of changing water into wine, John refers to this work as "the first of the signs given by Jesus" (John 2:11). Signs of what? What is a sign? I. de la Potterie answers: "Signs are symbolic acts by which Jesus reveals himself as Messiah and the Son of God."[1] When we are reading John's Gospel we have to pay attention not just to the literal meaning of the words but also to the symbolic meaning of the context. If we miss the symbolism of the events or signs that John recounts, we miss what he is trying to communicate.

Let us remind ourselves how symbols work in human society. The shamrock is a good example. If a visitor to planet Earth tried to understand, by undertaking botanical research, why people in New York, Dublin, London, and Sydney were wearing a sprig of a green, three-leaved plant on the feast of St. Patrick, our visitor would not have much success. To understand why people wear the shamrock the visitor will have to leave the botanical world and enter into the world of symbolism and learn there about St. Patrick's use of the shamrock to illustrate the mystery of the Blessed Trinity. We have to do the same when reading St. John's Gospel. For instance, while reflecting on the marriage feast at Cana, if we think only about the actual marriage that took place there and not about the symbolism of marriage as a sign of the covenant between God and his people, we will miss John's message. Similarly, if we think only about the amount of wine that Jesus made from the water (120 gallons!) and do not reflect on the meaning of this superabundance of wine as the sign of the kingdom, we will again be missing John's point. Word and symbol go hand in hand in John.

❧

The Seven Signs in John's Gospel

Scholars point out that there are seven major signs in John's Gospel and that the whole ministry of Jesus takes place between the first and the seventh sign. These signs are as follows:

1. The wedding feast at Cana (2:1–12)
2. The healing of the dying son (4:46–54)
3. The Sabbath healing at Bethesda (5:1–16)
4. The multiplication of loaves (6:1–15)
5. The Sabbath healing of the blind man (9:1–41)
6. The restoration of Lazarus to life (11:1–44)
7. The great hour of Jesus: his mother, the cross, the issue of blood and water from Jesus' side (19:25–37)[2]

Mary is present at the first sign in Cana and the last sign on Calvary. As Joseph Grassi comments: "Her presence is not incidental, but central in the first and last sign. Her name and presence open and close the first sign at Cana, as well as the last sign on the cross. In the first sign, the word "mother" is used four times and "woman" once; in the seventh sign, "mother" is likewise found four times and "woman" once. Joseph Grassi shows how these seven signs are interrelated: "signs 3 and 5 are Sabbath-day healings; signs 2 and 6 death-to-life themes; signs 1 and 7 complement each other as beginning and end. Linked together are Jesus' mother in both Jesus' hour (2:4; 19:27), the Cana wine and the bitter wine of the cross (2:1; 19:29, 30), the imperfect Cana water and the water/blood/Spirit from Christ's side."[3] In this chapter we will focus on the first and last signs. Is there a connection between Cana and Calvary? Should we understand the first sign of the wedding feast at Cana, in the light of the last sign of Jesus' crucifixion on Calvary? What do both signs tell us about Jesus and about Mary? Let us prayerfully read John's narrative of the wedding at Cana.

ℬ

Cana

Three days later there was a wedding at Cana in Galilee. The mother of Jesus was there, and Jesus and his disciples had also been invited. When they ran out of wine, since the wine provided for the wedding was all finished, the mother of Jesus said to him, "They have no wine." Jesus said, "Woman, why turn to me? My hour has not come yet." His mother said to the servants, "Do whatever he tells you." There were six stone water jars standing there, meant for the ablutions that are customary among the Jews: each could hold twenty or thirty gallons. Jesus said to the servants, "Fill the jars with water," and they filled them to the brim. "Draw out now," he told them, "and take it to the steward." They did this: the steward tasted the water, and it had turned into wine. Having no idea where it came from—only the servants who had drawn the water knew—the steward called the bridegroom and said, "People generally serve the best wine first, and keep the cheaper sort till the guests have plenty to drink; but you have kept the best wine till now." This was the first of the signs given by Jesus; it was given at Cana in Galilee. He let his glory be seen, and his disciples believed in him. After this he went down to Capernaum with his mother and the brothers, but they stayed there only a few days. (John 2:1–12)

Traditionally Catholics have used the Cana story to prove the efficacy of Mary's intercession. Her intercession is so powerful that Jesus even anticipated his hour for working miracles at her request. Before we draw any conclusions about the power of Mary's intercession we must ask ourselves how we move from the "historical facts" of the Cana story to the "symbolic meaning" of the story. We will find Mary's true role on the symbolic level.

The Wedding Guests

The first wedding guest mentioned in John's account is "the mother of Jesus." Mary, therefore, is an important guest. A very early tradition has it that she was the aunt of the bridegroom. John always refers to her as "the mother of Jesus." This was an honorific way of speaking. As Raymond Brown points out, "Among Arabs today the 'mother of X' is an honorable title for a woman who has been fortunate enough to have a son."[4] Next on the wedding list are Jesus and his disciples. They are the only other guests mentioned. The groom is mentioned only once, and the bride is not mentioned at all. The presumption is, of course, that there were quite a number of guests, since the wine ran out. This would have been a major humiliation for the young couple. The practice in those days was for the guests to provide most of the wine. Since Jesus and his disciples were too poor to buy wine, their failure to provide some may have been the cause of the

shortage.[5] That in itself would have been sufficient reason for
Mary to intervene with Jesus. Her intervention and the way Jesus
responded to her observation that "they have no wine" have been
understood in many different ways. Despite Jesus' apparent
refusal—"Woman why turn to me? My hour has not come yet"—
he proceeded to rescue the situation, providing an enormous
quantity of wine. The headwaiter was astounded and complained
to the bridegroom that he had done a rather foolish thing by
keeping the best wine to last.

    Those are the facts of the wedding at Cana. We must move,
however, from the factual to the symbolic. The facts must be considered, but the facts point to something else. As de la Potterie
says,

> It is for this reason that John is extremely precise, even in the
> concrete details of the life of Jesus; they prove themselves to
> be full of meaning because they revert to something more
> profound. This first level is of the utmost importance, because
> it enables the indispensable passage to the second level. We are
> thus confronted by John with a world of signs and symbols
> which evoke something else, a reality without which neither
> would be visible or accessible.[6]

What reality becomes visible or accessible through the facts of
the Cana story? How does the transition from fact to symbol take
place?

The Symbolic Meaning of Wedding Feast

Every detail in John's account moves from fact to symbol. Thus,
when Mary says to Jesus, "they have no wine," Jesus immediately
responds in terms of his messianic mission and says, "my hour
has not yet come." Wine, for Jesus, signified the new wine of salvation. The prophet Amos foretold: "The days are coming . . .
when the mountains will run with new wine and the hills all
flow with it" (9:13). Wine was the symbol of the messianic time,
the time of the deliverance of God's people. Since this wine will
flow only at the messianic hour, through Jesus' triumph, Jesus

says, "my hour has not yet come." Mary, however, didn't take this as a refusal. She immediately said to the servants, "Do whatever he tells you." Jesus then showed that he would not refuse his mother's request, because he told the servants to fill the six stone water jars with water. They held about 120 gallons in all. Thus, he provided wine in abundance for the feast. As the headwaiter said to the groom, "You have kept the best wine until last."

We have, then, four major symbols in John's short narrative: the wedding feast, the woman, the hour, and the abundance of wine.

Jesus worked "the first of his signs" in the context of a wedding feast. As Megan McKenna notes:

> In John's gospel the wedding feast, the place where food is shared, is a privileged place of revelation and a place of worship, liturgy, and preaching of the good news. The gift of faith is shared as surely as the food and drink. The wedding feast is the open door to the kingdom of peace and justice, the entrance used by the Messiah to come into the world. It is the place where the old promises start to become true in surprising ways.[7]

In the Old Testament God's redemption of his people is spoken of in terms of a wedding feast: "Like a young man marrying a virgin, your rebuilder will wed you, and as the bridegroom rejoices in his bride, so will your God rejoice in you" (Isa. 62:5). For other references to this biblical theme of the messianic nuptials, see Hos. 2:16–25; Jer. 2:1–2; 3:1, 6–12; Ezekiel 16; Isa. 50:1; 54:4–8. God's covenant with his people is symbolized as a nuptial union. Jesus himself uses the symbol of the wedding feast to speak about the kingdom: "The kingdom of heaven may be compared to a king who gave a feast for his son's wedding" (Matt. 22:1–14). On the symbolic level, then, we have to understand the wedding feast as the place where revelation will take place, where faith will be shared because the wedding feast itself is the sign of the new nuptials between God and his people, the sign of the new covenant which Christ will establish and proclaim when he takes the cup at the Last Supper, when "his hour" has come, and he says, "This cup is the new covenant in my blood which will be poured out for you" (Luke 22:20).

The wedding feast at Cana is a symbol of the nuptial of the new covenant. That is why John doesn't really tell us anything about any of the other guests, not even the bride. John is not really interested in the bride and groom and the other guests. The only names on his guest list are Mary and Jesus and Jesus' disciples. The wedding feast is the symbolic background to "the first of the signs which Jesus worked." Mary and her intervention with Jesus are at the center of this first sign. Jesus himself draws our attention to the centrality of Mary by addressing her not as "Mother" but as "Woman." Brown points out that in the whole of the Bible and ancient literature there is not a single example, apart from Cana and Calvary, of a son addressing his mother as "Woman."[8] In addressing her thus Jesus is drawing our attention to something new, something different about his mother. De la Potterie writes:

> We have to keep in mind that from this moment on Jesus "begins" to *manifest himself* as Messiah and, by that very fact, the relationship between him and Mary is no longer the same; it is no longer the simple relationship of a son to his mother. Jesus now takes upon himself another role (a messianic role); and, what is very important, in addressing his mother as "Woman," he *involves her* in his mission which is beginning. By this appellation, he places a certain distance between himself and their former relationship, that of mother–son, but, at the same time, he opens up a new perspective; and he entices her into accepting another relationship with him in the mystery of salvation, beyond the maternal and familial.[9]

From Mary's reaction to being addressed as "Woman" we can see that she entered wholeheartedly into this new relationship. She went to the servants at the wedding feast and said to them, "Do whatever he tells you." Despite our difficulties in understanding Jesus' enigmatic expression "Woman, what do you want from me? My hour has not yet come," we see that Mary understood them in such a way that she immediately began to prepare the "servants" to obey the instructions of Jesus. Indeed scholars point out that the words Mary uses—"Do whatever he tells you"—are very similar to the words the people of Israel used when they committed themselves to the covenant with God: "Whatever Yahweh has said, we will do" (Exod. 19:8). Mary, recalling the people's profession of faith in the Old Covenant, now exhorts the "servants" to have the same attitude toward Jesus that their ancestors had toward the God of the Covenant, to give Jesus their total obedience. Mary is already exercising her spiritual motherhood and preparing the servants, the disciples, to have complete trust in Jesus.

When we see Cana in this light, the behavior of Mary and Jesus begins to make sense. They actually took over. The young couple are well in the background. Mary takes the initiative, approaches Jesus, and then gives orders to the servants. Jesus at first seems to protest, but then he too gives orders to the servants—and all this without the knowledge of the couple. Why have Mary and Jesus taken over the running of the feast? Because in John's mind the real feast is the messianic one, where Jesus is the bridegroom. This understanding was well expressed by St. Bernard when he wrote:

> This was a great sign of the divine force and power to change water into wine solely by his will. But in this miracle another change is significant for us, which is also a work of the finger of God: and this is so much the better and more salutary for us: we are all called to the spiritual wedding feast where Jesus Christ, our Lord, is the Bridegroom.[10]

In the very next chapter of the Gospel, John the Baptist will call Jesus "the bridegroom."

Jesus is the true bridegroom at the messianic wedding. His transforming presence effects not just the physical miracle of changing water into wine but the symbolic miracle of changing the water for Jewish purification into the life-giving wine of the

New Covenant. The abundant supply of the miraculous "best wine" is a sign to his disciples. John says, "He let his glory be seen and his disciples believed in him." Mary believed without the sign. As Kathleen Coyle writes:

> The fourth evangelist describes Mary's response to Jesus in such a way that her faith is never in doubt. Without witnessing any miraculous signs, she knows what he will do. She demonstrates that her relationship to Jesus is based on her faith in him, and not merely on their biological relationship. His death, to which the Cana sign points, is a death his mother will witness and remember. We note the parallel to the seventh sign, where Jesus obeys the Father's will and drinks the cup of suffering prepared by his Father. Mary's continuing role within the community is that of a concerned mother, pointing in obedience to Jesus' word, understood now in the light of his death. As intercessor, she continues to request the new wine of the Spirit for the Church.[11]

ℰ

Calvary

The second time Mary appears in John's Gospel is on Calvary. He describes the scene succinctly:

> Near the cross of Jesus stood his mother and his mother's sister Mary the wife of Clopas, and Mary of Magdala. Seeing his mother and the disciple whom he loved standing near her, Jesus said to his mother, "Woman, this is your son." Then to the disciple he said, "This is your mother." And from that hour the disciple took her into his own home. (John 19:26–27)

Aware of the symbolic level on which John writes, we have to pay particular attention to this scene. In the first place, none of the other Gospels records that Mary was on Calvary and that Jesus spoke to her. This is surprising, because Matthew and especially Luke have a great interest in Mary's role as mother in the infancy of Jesus. Why did they not record her presence on Cal-

vary? We are also struck by the fact that John's Gospel was written about sixty years after the death of Jesus. The writer tells us
that he did not record everything that Jesus did and said: "The
whole world would not contain the number of books that would
be written" (John 21:25), "but these are recorded so that you may
believe that Jesus is the Christ, the Son of God, and that believing this you have life through his name" (20:31). John is making
it very clear, then, that Mary's presence on Calvary and Jesus'
words to her are recorded so that we might believe. We cannot
pass over this presence of Mary and these words of Jesus as if they
had nothing to do with us. They have everything to do with us
and our salvation. The phrase "seeing his mother" is very significant. What does Jesus see when he sees his mother? He sees the
mother of his disciple. The first time Jesus spoke to his mother in
John's Gospel at Cana he said, "My hour has not yet come." By
his hour he meant his hour of exaltation on the cross, when he
would accomplish the work the Father gave him to do: "When I
am lifted up I will draw all to myself." Now his hour has come,
the hour of his victory over Satan, sin, and death. It is in this
hour that he again speaks to his mother.

"Revelation Schema"

As he looks at Mary from the cross, he declares what he sees in
her, namely, a new maternity, a spiritual maternity of his disciples. Scripture scholars refer to this passage as a "revelation
schema." Jesus is revealing something new about his mother. He
proclaims to us what he sees in his mother so that we can believe.
Faith is seeing with the eyes of Jesus. As Jesus looks on his mother
from the cross, he sees not just his own physical mother; he sees
the spiritual mother of his disciple, of his church, which is coming to birth through his death and resurrection. De la Potterie
illustrates how John uses this literary device, the "revelation
schema," by pointing to John the Baptist's recognition of Jesus.
"The next day, he saw Jesus coming towards him and said, 'Look,
there is the lamb of God that takes away the sin of the world'"

(John 1:29). We see four elements in this "revelation schema": (1) Jesus is approaching; (2) John looks at him; (3) John calls for attention with the words "Look," and (4) John declares what he sees: "the lamb of God."[12] John the Baptist reveals that the stranger passing by is none other than the Messiah of Israel. That is revelation. In the same way Jesus reveals that his mother is none other than the mother of the disciple. That is revelation. Jesus sees in his mother a new maternity, a spiritual maternity. He proclaims what he sees: "He is your son." His very last word to his mother is about her new relationship with his disciple.

Having seen a new reality, a new motherhood, in his own mother, Jesus then turns his gaze toward his disciple. What does he see in the disciple? Yes, he sees the disciple whom he loves, faithful at the foot of the cross. But he sees something else. He sees his brother. He sees one who has the same mother as himself. And he declares what he sees with the everlasting, creative word of God: "She is your mother." He sees in his disciple so much of himself that he can say, "Now we have the same mother," now we are truly brothers. Through that creative word of Jesus the disciple comes into a new relationship with his master, and the sign of that new relationship is that both are sons of the same mother. Jesus in his humanity is the son of Mary; the disciple in his redeemed humanity is the son of Mary.

How does the disciple respond? "From that hour the disciple took her to his own home." This interpretation of the Greek text of John's Gospel is being reconsidered by many scholars today. John McHugh writes:

> If we take careful notice of John's vocabulary, a more meaningful rendering emerges. In the Fourth Gospel, the verb *lambanō* has two senses. When applied to material things, it means simply "to take hold of," "to pick up," "to grasp," etc. (e.g. 6:11; 12:13; 13:12; 19:23, 40); when applied to immaterial things, it means "to accept" or "to welcome," usually as a gift from God (e.g. his witness, 3:11; his word, 17:8; his Spirit, 14:17; 1Jn 2:27). Secondly, the words *eis ta idia*, which cer-

tainly can mean "to one's own home" (in a purely physical sense), can also mean "among one's own spiritual possessions" (compare John 8:44 and 15:19, in the Greek). The phrase is found in the prologue with this double meaning of "physical home" and "spiritual possession," and in close conjunction with the verb "to accept or welcome." "He came to *what was his own* . . . and to all who *accepted* him, he gave the power to become children of God" (John 1:12–13). John 19:27 seems to demand a translation which includes both the purely physical and the deeper, spiritual sense. "And from that hour the disciple took her into his own home and accepted her as his own mother, as part of the spiritual legacy bequeathed to him by the Lord."[13]

A growing number of scripture scholars accept this interpretation of John's action. He took her to his own house, but more profoundly he accepted her, he welcomed her into his own life as his mother. That is the response he made to Jesus' words, "She is your mother."

The Beloved Disciple

Who is that disciple whom Jesus loved? Traditionally we always say John. But, if John was the name of the disciple, why didn't the Gospel say so? The Gospel of John is full of names: Mary the wife of Clophas, Mary Magdala, Martha and Mary and Lazarus. But John's Gospel doesn't name the mother of Jesus or the beloved disciple. The Gospel doesn't say "John"; it says "the disciple Jesus loves." Who is this disciple whom Jesus loves? Maybe we should put the question this way: Is there any disciple whom Jesus doesn't love? Maybe I should put the question directly to you: Are you a disciple whom Jesus loves? What does Jesus see when he sees the disciple whom he loves? He sees the new reality of redemption; he sees someone whom he calls his brother or sister; he sees someone to whom he says, "She is your mother." If you are a disciple whom Jesus loves, then Jesus says to you, "She is your mother."

The great Protestant scripture scholar Martin Dibelius wrote: "The beloved disciple is the person of faith, who has no need of proof (20:8). He is the witness to the mystery of the cross (19:35), and at the foot of the cross he becomes the son of Jesus' mother, thus representing other disciples who, in their relationship with God, have become brothers of Jesus.[14]

Max Thurian, another great non-Catholic scholar writes:

The disciple designated as "he whom Jesus loved" is without question the personification of the perfect disciple, of the true faithful follower of Christ, of the believer who has received the Spirit. It is not a question here of Jesus' special affection for one of his apostles, but a symbolic personification of fidelity to the Lord.[15]

Jesus entrusts his beloved disciple to the maternal care of his mother. This is a clear sign that Jesus is not just trying to find a home for his mother after his death. This is not simply a private, domestic arrangement that Jesus is making for his mother. He is entrusting to her a new responsibility. From now on she will be the mother, the true, spiritual mother of his disciples. He has spoken God's word to her: "He is your son." Mary must now live by that word. We know how Mary received the first word that God spoke to her when he invited her to be the mother of his Son. She said, "Let it be done unto me according to your word." Now the word of God is addressed to her again, the very last word that her own son Jesus spoke to her on earth, and that word says, "He is your son." Mary's response is the same: Let it be done unto me according to your word. Through the power of the word of God Mary becomes the mother of the disciple, she becomes the mother of all the disciples. Her God-given mission from now on is to be the mother of the disciples. The beloved disciple too receives a new mission from Jesus. To him Jesus says, "She is your mother." Jesus' very last word to his disciple entrusts Mary to him as his own mother. The disciple must live by that word of God spoken by Jesus. We see how he responds. "From that hour the disciple took her into his own home." Receiving Mary as his own mother from the hands of Jesus on the cross is the last thing that the beloved disciple did before Jesus proclaimed, "It is fulfilled" (John 19:30). It is what every beloved disciple must do. Every disciple must live by the word of God which proclaims, "She is your mother," just as Mary now lives by the word that declares to her, "He is your son," "She is your daughter."

Reflecting on Mary's presence on Calvary the Second Vatican Council said:

> Thus the Blessed Virgin advanced in her pilgrimage of faith, and faithfully persevered in her union with her Son until she at the cross, in keeping with the divine plan (see Jn 19:25), suffering deeply with her only begotten Son, associating herself with his sacrifice in her mother's heart, and lovingly consenting to the immolation of this victim who was born of her. Finally, she was given by the same Christ Jesus dying on the cross as a mother to his disciple, with these words: "Woman, this is your Son" (John 19:26–27). (*Lumen Gentium* 58)

The mother of Jesus, his faithful disciple to the end, is the *mater dolorosa*, the Mother of Sorrows, who shared in the immense and bitter sufferings of her Son as he offered himself for our salvation. Just as she consented to God's plan at the Annunciation, so she consented to the fulfillment of that plan on Calvary. She had heard her Son teach, "No one can have greater love than to lay down his life for his friends" (John 15:13). If Jesus is ready to die for us, Mary too would have been willing to lay down her life for us. In fact, in the Christian tradition Mary is honored as Queen of Martyrs. The church recognizes that Mary so associated herself with Jesus on the cross that she suffered in her heart what he was suffering in his body. Mary became the mother of "the beloved disciple" in the awesome hour of the crucifixion of Jesus. As Pope John Paul II says: "This 'new motherhood of Mary,' generated by faith, is *the fruit of the 'new' love* which came to definitive maturity in her at the foot of the Cross, through her sharing in the redemptive love of her son" (*Redemptoris mater* 23).

In John's Gospel Mary the mother of Jesus is the woman of

faith. She is the first to believe in Jesus before he worked any signs, as we saw at Cana. Her faith rested not on "signs" but on the word of God. That is why, when all seemed lost, Mary's faith in her Son brought her to the foot of his cross. Her presence on Calvary, in the darkest hour of her life and the life of Jesus, proclaims for all time the victory of God over evil. We do not know what went through Mary's mind at the foot of her Son's cross. But we believe, in the words of the Second Vatican Council, that on Calvary Mary "associated herself with his sacrifice in her mother's heart" (*Lumen Gentium* 57). Because of that association, because of her willing participation in his life and work, Jesus speaks the life-giving words to each disciple: She is your mother.

Mary in the Early Church

𝒢𝔞 THE NEW TESTAMENT PRESENTS MARY as a principal participant in each of the main mysteries of the Lord's life and work: She was the willing and joyful collaborator in the mystery of the incarnation: "Oh yes, let it be done unto me according to your word!" Through her intervention at Cana, Jesus performed his first sign, "and his disciples believed in him." She stood at the foot of the cross, in "the hour" of Jesus and heard Jesus commit the beloved disciple to her maternal care as her own son, and at Pentecost she was present with the disciples when the Holy Spirit came. She was, therefore, present at the physical birth of Christ, and she was present at the mystical birth of Christ, the birth of the church. Tradition will begin to see a correlation between her participation in the physical birth and her participation in the mystical birth.

The question we want to reflect on now is: What did the generations after the New Testament writers think about Mary? How did they understand her role? What did the bishops and theologians of those early days teach? If you, for instance, were living in Antioch in the year A.D. 100, what would you have heard the bishop of that community say about Mary? Antioch was the first Gentile community of Christians. Paul and Barnabas, we are

[I am basing this chapter on the third volume of Bertrand Buby's excellent trilogy, *Mary of Galilee* (New York: Alba House, 1994). The quotations from the fathers of the church that I use are taken from this volume and can be found under the name of the individual father in this volume.]

told, preached the gospel for eighteen months in Antioch. St. Peter also preached the gospel in that city. It was in Antioch that the followers of Christ were first called "Christians." Thus, the church community in Antioch was deeply rooted in the apostolic ministry of both St. Peter and St. Paul.

ℰ

St. Ignatius of Antioch
A.D. 110

St. Ignatius, martyred around the year 110 was the third bishop of Antioch. He was reputed to have heard John the Apostle preach. As a successor of the apostles in the church at Antioch, what did Bishop Ignatius have to say about Mary? New questions were being asked about Jesus, questions that Paul did not have to address. Paul, for instance, proclaimed that Jesus Christ is Lord and that salvation comes through accepting him as Lord and Savior. At the time of Ignatius, about thirty or forty years after the death of Paul, some believers who had accepted Christ were beginning to understand Jesus in quite different ways. Some could not accept that Jesus was really a human being. They held that Jesus, the Son of God, the Savior, only *appeared* to be a human being. They are called docetists. They had a very poor esteem of "the flesh." In fact, they despised the "flesh." They could not, therefore, abide the thought of a true incarnation. How could God enter into despicable human flesh? The very thought was not just abhorrent but blasphemous.

It was against this background of docetism, the doctrine that Jesus only appeared to be a human being, that Ignatius preached and taught. What aspects of the gospel did Ignatius emphasize to combat these errors? He emphasized the very truth that these heretics were denying—the true humanity of Jesus. And where did Jesus get his humanity? From his mother. Ignatius writes:

For indeed our God Jesus the Christ was borne in the womb of Mary according to the divine plan, of the seed of David but also of a holy spirit. He was born and was baptized in order that by his suffering he might purify the water. Now the virginity of Mary was hidden from the prince of this world, as was also her offspring, and the death of the Lord; three mysteries loudly shouted out, which, however, were wrought in silence and, yet, have been revealed to us. (*Letter to the Ephesians*)

Ignatius is restating in vigorous and clear language the faith that he had received from the apostles and which he is defending against the attacks of heretics. He uses strong and colorful language to talk about these heretics:

There are some [false teachers] who are going about with malicious deceit while hearing the name of Christ. They are doing things offensive to God. You should avoid them like ferocious beasts. Indeed they are rabid dogs, whose bite is hard to heal. (*Letter to the Ephesians*)

Strong language! But much was at stake. The very mystery of the incarnation of Christ, the central mystery of our faith, was at stake. These heretics accepted Jesus as Savior but denied that he had come in the flesh. Ignatius had to stress Christ's coming in the flesh. Christ came in the flesh through his virgin mother. He came virginally. As Ignatius says, "He comes from both Mary and God. Because of the former he suffers, because of the latter he is impassable, Jesus Christ our Lord." His virginal conception, Ignatius tells us, is a mystery hidden from "the prince of this world."

Writing to another church, the Trallians, Ignatius says:

Close your ears then, should anyone speak to you without speaking about Jesus Christ, who descended from the family of David, and who was born from Mary. He was truly born of a human being, he ate and drank, he was persecuted under Pontius Pilate, indeed crucified and died, and raised by the Father who, since we are like to him, will also raise us up in

> Jesus Christ; we who believe in him and without whom we have no true life. (*Letter to the Trallians*)

In this passage we see the beginnings of our creed. The fact that Jesus was truly a man, truly a son of David, truly flesh and blood had to be emphasized against the attacks of those who believed that God could not come in the flesh. What better way to achieve all this than to make sure that all the faithful, when they heard about Christ, heard that he "was born of the virgin Mary"? Since the incarnation of the Son of God as Mary's son is at the very heart of our Christian faith, Mary is at the center of our faith. It has been rightly said that Mary is not the center—Christ is the center—but she is at the center. Whenever there is an error about Christ, Mary will be invoked as a witness to the truth: the truth of his humanity, because she bore him in her womb, and the truth of his divinity, because she conceived him virginally through the Holy Spirit.

We see, then, in the teaching of this early Christian bishop, writing only a few years after the appearance of John's Gospel, and thirty years after Luke's Gospel, a robust reminder of the role of Mary in the history of salvation. The emerging heresies concerning Jesus forced Ignatius to stress Mary's role as his virginal mother.

St. Justin Martyr
A.D. 100–165

The first Christian philosopher was Justin Martyr. He lived from around 100 to 165. He was born in Nabulus in Samaria. He was converted to Christ and became known as the first apologist for the faith. As Justin reflected on the faith, on the Scriptures, he saw a parallel between the role of Eve and the role of Mary. He writes:

> He became man by the Virgin, in order that the disobedience which proceeded from the serpent might receive its destruc-

tion in the same manner in which it derived its origin. For Eve, who was a virgin and undefiled, having conceived by the word of the Serpent, brought forth disobedience and death. But the Virgin Mary received faith and joy, when the angel Gabriel announced good tidings to her that the Spirit of the Lord would come upon her, and the power of the most high would overshadow her; wherefore also the Holy One begotten of her is the Son of God; and she replied, "Be it done unto me according to your word." And by her has He been born, to whom we have proved so many scriptures refer, and by whom God destroys both the serpent and those angels and men who are like him; but works deliverance from death to those who repent of their wickedness and believe in Him. (*Dialogue with Trypho*)

Christian reflection on the role of Mary has now begun in earnest. What Eve was in the Old Testament Mary is in the New Testament. According to Cardinal Newman, Justin's teaching on this parallel between Eve and Mary was a fundamental theological insight, a Mariological insight. We do not know whether Justin was the first to see this parallel between Eve and Mary or whether this was pointed out to him when he was educated in the faith. It is quite possible that the church community in which he was baptized was already using this parallel in its catechetical instruction of its members.

ॐ

St. Irenaeus, Bishop of Lyons
A.D. *140-202*

This parallel between Eve and Mary would receive its magisterial development in the writings of another early bishop and martyr, St. Irenaeus, bishop of Lyons. Irenaeus was born in Smyrna (Turkey) in A.D. 140 and died in Lyons in 202, still very close to apostolic times. He had for his teacher St. Polycarp, who was, according to Cardinal Newman, an associate of John the Apostle.

Irenaeus, from the church in the East, brought the apostolic faith to the West. He is, therefore, a very important witness to the development of the faith of the church. What did Bishop Irenaeus teach about Mary?

Irenaeus's major insight was his doctrine of recapitulation. Whatever has gone wrong in human history has been taken up, restored, and redeemed in Christ. Christ becomes the head of the new humanity. He is the new Adam. But Adam, the old head of the human race, had a collaborator in the person of Eve. She became, as Scripture says, "the mother of all the living." Jesus, the new Adam, head of the new humanity, has a collaborator in the person of Mary. As Jesus parallels Adam, so Mary parallels Eve. Mary is the new Eve in God's new creation. This teaching, acknowledged in our day by the Second Vatican Council (*Lumen Gentium* 56), would become a major theme in the development of the church's teaching on Mary. Because Irenaeus introduced this teaching, he has been called the first "mariologist." Let us look at some of his basic texts:

> In accordance with this design Mary the Virgin is found obedient, saying, "Behold the handmaid of the Lord, be it done unto me according to thy word." But Eve was disobedient; for she did not obey when she was yet a virgin. And even as she, having indeed a husband, Adam, but being nevertheless as yet a virgin (for in Paradise "they were both naked, and were not ashamed" inasmuch as they, having been created a short time previously, had no understanding of the procreation of children; for it was necessary that they should first come to adult age, and then multiply from that time onward), having become disobedient, was made the cause of death, both to herself and the whole human race; so also did Mary, having a man betrothed (to her), and being nevertheless a virgin, by yielding obedience, become the cause of salvation, both to herself and the whole human race.

The contrast between Eve and Mary is clear: Eve, by disobedience, became the cause of death; Mary, by obedience, became the cause of salvation. If Bishop Irenaeus writes that "Mary became the cause of salvation for herself and the whole human race," we can be certain that he frequently preached this doctrine to his people. We can imagine ourselves in Lyons in the year 200, listening to Irenaeus preaching on the mystery of the incarnation. He is preaching about the angel Gabriel's announcement to Mary and Mary's response. When he comes to comment on her words, "Let it be done unto me according to your word," he breaks into a comparison between Eve and Mary. He develops the parallel. He leaves us, like a good preacher, with this phrase ringing in our ears: "Mary by her obedience became the cause of salvation for herself and the whole human race." Scripture says that "sin entered the world through one man and through sin death" (Rom. 5:12). Sin and death entered the world through man, through Adam. Reflecting on how sin and death came into the world and how salvation came into the world, Irenaeus parallels the role of Eve and Mary.

This parallel, full of theological insight, has unfortunately not functioned in history for the liberation of women. Some theologians would agree with Kathleen Coyle, who writes in her excellent book *Mary in the Christian Tradition:* "Because a system of domination has biased the whole range of theological symbols, traditional marian symbols such as Mary the New Eve, and the New Adam–New Eve typology have functioned, however unconsciously, to keep women oppressed."[1] Instead of being lined up with Mary, in the new creation, women have been lined up with Eve, in the old creation, and from this association they have been denounced and often rejected. Strangely, men were not simply associated with the old Adam.

ℱᵋ

Apocryphal Writings

During the first 150 years of the church's history, while the writings of Ignatius, Justin, and Irenaeus were guiding the faithful in the true faith, other writings also appeared. These writings are called the Apocrypha. These writings claimed to be by the apostles or one of the early disciples. The best known and most influential of these writings was the *Protevangelium of James,* which claimed to have James, the "brother of the Lord," as its author. This book, claiming as it does to have a member of Christ's family as author, tells us about Mary's childhood: about her parents, Joachim and Anna, about her birth and her presentation in the Temple. We owe the tradition that Jesus was born in a cave to this book. Another tradition which we owe to the Book of James concerns St. Joseph. He has always been depicted in Christian art as an old man, much older than Mary. The church, however, did not accept these apocryphal writings as part of the New Testament. Yet they were quite influential in the early church. We see this from our liturgy. We celebrate the feast of Sts. Joachim and Anna (16 August); the feast of Our Lady's birthday (8 September); the feast of her Presentation in the temple (21 November). The *Protevangelium of James* was also the first writing to clearly state Mary's perpetual virginity. As early, then, as A.D. 130–150 Christians were familiar with this doctrine. Ignatius, writing well before the *Protevangelium of James* was written, had emphasized the "virgin birth," but the author of the apocryphal book emphasizes Mary's perpetual virginity.

The *Protevangelium of James* was very popular with the early Christians because it purported to answer the questions people had on their minds: What kind of person was Mary? What was her childhood like? And her parents? And Joseph, her husband? And what was the childhood of Jesus like? How did he mix with other children? Did he show any signs of his extraordinary power as a boy? The New Testament does not answer any of these questions, and the church has never based its teaching on the apocryphal writings. "There are over one hundred early manuscripts of this apocryphal text! This demonstrates the interest and curiosity of the early Christians about the earliest stages of Jesus' life and his hidden development that are only hinted at in the Infancy Narratives of Matthew and Luke."[2]

In the first 150 years of the history of the church we find that interest in Mary is quite widespread. A bishop like St. Ignatius appealed to Mary's virginal conception to defend the humanity of Jesus; a philosopher like Justin highlighted the parallel between Mary and Eve; the bishop St. Irenaeus from the East brought his interest in Mary to the West and developed his theology of "recapitulation," in which Christ is presented as the New Adam and Mary the New Eve. He developed the parallel between Mary and Eve and concluded that "Mary became the cause of salvation for herself and the whole human race." At the same time, the apocryphal writings were very popular and quite widespread. All the while the Christian faith was spreading throughout the pagan Roman Empire. The three writers whom we have looked at, Ignatius, Justin, and Irenaeus, were all martyred for their faith in Christ. They witnessed through their life and death to their faith in Jesus; they also witnessed, through their preaching, teaching, and writing to their belief that the Virgin Mary played a very significant role as the New Eve in the work of our salvation. The New Testament itself, especially the writings of Luke and John, provide us with the revealed doctrine on Mary's role in the life and work of Christ; the bishops and theologians who followed on from the apostles defended and developed what was handed on in the Scriptures.

℅

Origen
A.D. *185–254*

Origen is regarded as the great intellectual giant of the early church. He was born of Christian parents in Alexandria in Egypt in the year 185. His father was martyred in the year 202. He was the most original thinker and commentator on the Scriptures. The following passage gives us a flavor of how he saw Mary:

> We may therefore venture to say that the flower of all the Scriptures are the Gospels, and the flower of the Gospels is

that according to John, the sense of which no one is able to receive who had not reclined upon the breast of Jesus, or who has not received from Jesus, Mary to be his Mother also. Yea, such and so great must he needs become who is to be another John. As John was, so too must he be shown to be Jesus, by Jesus. For, if in the judgement of those whose sentiments are sound concerning Mary, there be no Son of Mary save Jesus, and Jesus says to his Mother, "Behold your son," and not, "Behold he too is your son,"—it is the same as though He said, Behold he is Jesus whom you have brought forth. For whosoever is perfect, himself no longer lives, but Christ lives in him, and since Christ lives in him, of him it is said to Mary, Behold your son, Christ. How great an understanding, then, do we not need, to be able to find out the word that lies hidden among the treasures covered over by the shell of the bare letter—that letter which every one who chances to see it may read, and which is heard by all who lend their bodily ears to hear it. But he who would properly understand, should be able to say with truth. We have the mind of Christ, that we may know the things that are given us from God. (*Commentary on John*)

In Origen's understanding of the word "Behold your son," Jesus is so identifying himself with his disciple, with each of his disciples, that he is declaring the disciple to be himself. His expression is difficult, but his meaning is clear: "As John was, so too must he be shown to be Jesus, by Jesus." In simple language Origen is saying that since Jesus was the only son of Mary, if Jesus says John is her son he is saying that John in some way has become Jesus. Jesus and John are one; Jesus and his disciples are one. Because of this unity and identification Mary sees just her own Son in each of the disciples. Just imagine the effect of this teaching on people in Egypt around the year A.D. 230. Christians are still a small, persecuted minority. They would have welcomed this good news. Not only were they redeemed by Jesus but each of them, through the Lord's own indwelling, was Jesus. And to each of them Jesus said, "Behold your mother." Here we are at the very heart of Christian devotion to Mary. If Jesus so dwells in the true disciple that the disciple himself is Jesus, what disciple would not welcome the words "Behold your mother"? And what disciple would not do as John did, "From that moment the disciple took her to himself"?

℘

St. Athanasius of Alexandria
A.D. *295–373*

We want to introduce now St. Athanasius, another great Egyptian from Alexandria. A convert to the faith, he became a deacon and acted as secretary to Bishop Alexander during the Council of Nicaea in A.D. 325. Mention of that council reminds us that controversy was raging in the church at that time. A priest by the name of Arius, a devout and ascetical man, taught a doctrine about Christ that caused great division in the church. St. John's Gospel opens with the words: "In the beginning was the Word: the Word was with God and the Word was God. . . . The Word became flesh." The church believes that the Word, the second person of the Holy Trinity, is God, equal to the Father. Arius denied this. He taught that the Word existed before all other creatures but was created by the Father. The Word was not of "the same substance" as the Father. In other words, the Word was not God and the Word made flesh, Jesus Christ, was not God. The first general council of the church was held in Nicaea (in modern-day Turkey not far from Istanbul) in the year 325 to deal with this heretical teaching about Christ. This council condemned the teaching of Arius and presented the Catholic faith in a creed, the Nicene Creed, which we still say at Sunday Mass. In the Nicene Creed we say, "We believe in one Lord Jesus Christ, the only Son of God, eternally begotten of the Father, God from God, Light from Light, true God from true God, begotten not made, of one Being with the Father." Jesus Christ is the Son of God. He is divine as well as human. That is the mystery of the incarnation.

St. Athanasius was the great opponent of Arianism, the greatest champion of the divinity of Christ. When he became bishop
of Alexandria he suffered exile on five separate occasions because
of his defense of the true faith. This great champion of the divinity of Jesus was also a great devotee of the Mother of Jesus, proof
to all that devotion to Mary enhances rather than takes away
from devotion to Jesus. In a lyrical passage Athanasius addresses
Mary:

> Truly, O noble Virgin, you are great and above all greatness;
> who indeed can compare with your greatness; O dwelling
> place of the Word of God? With whom shall I compare you
> among all creatures? You are evidently greater than all of
> them. O Ark of the covenant surrounded totally and purely on
> all sides with gold! You are the Ark containing all gold, the
> receptacle of the true manna, that is human and wherein the
> divinity resides. Shall I not compare you with the fecund
> earth and its fruits? You surpass them. For it is written. "The
> earth is the footstool for my feet" (Is 66:1). Indeed in you you
> bear both the feet and head and entire body of a perfect God.
> Even if I speak of the highest heaven it will not compare to
> you; for it is written, "Heaven is my throne" (Is 66:1). For you
> are the dwelling place of God. Should I speak of the angels and
> the archangels, you are greater than they; for angels and
> archangels serve with fear the one who is contained within
> you, nor do they dare to speak in his presence, with whom
> you speak freely. If I speak of the great Cherubim, you excel
> even them; the Cherubim carry the throne of God while you
> carry God within your arms. If I speak of the Seraphim, you
> are greater still; they indeed cover their face with their wings
> not having perfect glory, while you not only contemplate the
> face, but kiss the sacred mouth and nourish it with your
> breasts. (*De Virginitate*)

This magnificent passage shows the depth of the love and
devotion in the heart of Athanasius for the Virgin Mary. But as
well as pouring forth his own devotion Athanasius continued to
develop the Marian theology that he had received. He was among
the first theologians to call Mary "*Theotokos,*" Mother of God. He

developed the parallelism between Eve and Mary. He was a stout defender of the perpetual virginity of Mary. His argument is still cogent for us today:

> If Mary would have had another son, the Savior would not have neglected her nor would he have confided his mother to another person; indeed she had not become the mother of another. Mary, moreover, would not have abandoned her own sons to live with another, for she fully realized a mother never abandons her spouse nor her children. And since she continued to remain a virgin even after the birth of the Lord, he gave her as mother to the disciple, even though she was not his mother; he confided her to John because of his great purity of conscience and because of her intact virginity. (*De Virginitate*)

Athanasius, the greatest defender of the divinity of Christ, was also the most ardent devotee of the mother of Christ. In him we find a perfect harmony between doctrine and devotion. What God has revealed to us in the Scriptures, concerning the mother of Jesus, he revealed for our salvation. Athanasius, who faithfully lived every word concerning Jesus and his relationship with Jesus, also lived every word concerning Mary and his relationship with Mary. No one could claim that Athanasius's devotion to Mary obscured the person of her Son. Rather, it was the glory and the munificence of God, manifested in Jesus, which revealed the true nature of the gift of Mary to the church. Those who were formed by the preaching, teaching, and writing of Athanasius would have had a deep faith in the divinity of Jesus and a warm devotion to the mother of Jesus, their mother.

❧

St. Ambrose
A.D. *339–397*

While Christians in the Eastern Church were being formed in this deep, Christ-centered theology of Athanasius, with its concomitant Marian doctrine and devotion, what was happening in the church in the West? St. Ambrose, bishop of Milan, gives us the answer. Ambrose was born in 339 and died in 397. While he was governor of northern Italy in 374, he was chosen by the people to be the bishop of Milan. At that time he was still a catechumen. He was baptized and within a week he was ordained priest and bishop. He was destined to become one of the greatest bishops of the Western church. He set himself the task of teaching the people the true faith. Basing all his teaching and preaching on the Scriptures and the Nicene Creed, Ambrose developed a Christ-centered theology. Like Athanasius, whose writings he studied, Ambrose was the great defender of the divinity of Christ. Lack of faith in the true incarnation of the Son of God was prevalent among certain groups. He writes:

> There are not enough hours in the day for me to recite even the names of all the various sects of heretics. But what is contrary to all of them is the general belief that Christ is the Son of God, eternally from the Father, and born of the Virgin Mary. . . . Since God must ever be eternal, He receives the mysteries of the Incarnation not as divided but as one: for both are one, and He is one in both, that is, in His divinity and in His Body. He is not one from the Father and another from the Virgin, but the same in one way from the Father and a different way from the Virgin. (*The Mystery of the Lord's Incarnation*)

Ambrose learned, through refuting the heresies of his time, that one cannot defend the divinity of Christ without at the same time proclaiming that the mother of Christ is truly the mother of God. Ambrose was the first theologian in the Western church to call Mary by the title *Mater Dei,* Mother of God. He was the defender of Mary's perpetual virginity. He writes, "Since Christ was born from the womb of the Virgin, nevertheless he preserved the enclosure of her sexual chastity and the untouched seal of her virginity." But Ambrose also developed new insights into the meaning and significance of Mary's vocation as mother of the Savior. He saw Mary as "Mother of the Church." Commenting on the woman in the apocalypse, he writes:

By the woman here we may also understand the Blessed Virgin Mary, because she is the Mother of the Church, for she brought forth Him who is Head of the Church, and is herself the daughter of the Church, since she is the greatest member of the Church. The dragon, then, stood before the woman, that on her giving birth he might devour her Son; because at the outset of Christ's birth the dragon had the intention of slaying Him by means of Herod his minister. He stands also before the woman, that is to say, the Church, in order to destroy by temptation to evil those whom by baptism she brings forth to God. (*Commentary on the Apocalypse*)

We see a constant clarification of Mary's role in the mystery of Christ. She is his mother; she conceived him virginally, through the power of the Holy Spirit, and she remained forever a virgin; she is being hailed not just as mother of Jesus but also as Mother of God, because Jesus her Son is the Son of God. She is the mother of the disciple, the mother of all disciples. She is, in fact, in the words of Ambrose "the Mother of the Church."

ℰ

St. Jerome
A.D. *347–420*

St. Jerome is another great father of the church. He was a renowned Scripture scholar, who translated the Hebrew Scriptures into Latin; he also translated the Greek New Testament into Latin. His familiarity with the biblical languages of Hebrew, Aramaic, and Greek equipped him for his life's work of expounding the Scriptures and defending the faith. Woe betide anyone who, in Jerome's view, deviated from the true faith, as the hapless Helvidius discovered. Helvidius denied the perpetual virginity of Mary. In launching his defense of her perpetual virginity Jerome prayed:

I must call upon the Holy Spirit to express His meaning by my mouth and defend the virginity of the Blessed Mary. I must

call upon the Lord Jesus to guard the sacred lodging of the
womb in which He abode from all suspicion of sexual intercourse. And I must also entreat God the Father to show that
the mother of His Son, who was mother before she was bride,
continued a Virgin after her son was born. (*Treatise on Mary's
Perpetual Virginity*)

This devout introduction does not prevent Jerome from
engaging in ridicule and sarcasm. For instance, referring to Helvidius's method of defending his position that Mary did not
remain a virgin after the birth of Jesus, he writes scornfully: "To
defend his position he piles up text upon text, waves his sword
like a blind-folded gladiator, rattles his noisy tongue, and ends up
with wounding no one but himself."

Helvidius was dealing with a real question. Who are the people called in the Gospel "his brothers and sisters"? If they were
his blood brothers and sisters this would mean that Mary had
other children after the birth of Jesus. (Some Christians today
still use this argument to oppose the Catholic doctrine of Mary's
perpetual virginity.) Jerome argued that, according to the lin-
guistic logic of Helvidius, it could be argued that Joseph was the
true father of Jesus:

It is clear that our Lord's brethren bore the name in the same
way that Joseph was called his father: "Your father and I have
sought you sorrowing." It was His mother who said this, not
the Jews. The Evangelist himself relates that His father and
mother were marvelling at the things which were spoken concerning Him, and there are similar passages which we have
already quoted in which Joseph and Mary are called his parents. Seeing that you have been foolish enough to persuade
yourself that the Greek manuscripts are corrupt, you will perhaps plead the diversity of readings. I therefore come to the
Gospel of John, and there it is plainly written, "Philip found
Nathaniel, and said to him, 'We have found him of whom
Moses in the Law, and the prophets all wrote, Jesus of
Nazareth, the son of Joseph.'" You will certainly find this in
your manuscript. Now tell me, how is Jesus the son of Joseph

when it is clear that He was begotten of the Holy Spirit? Was Joseph his true father? Dull as you are, you will not venture to say that. Was he his reputed father? If so, let the same rule be applied to them when they are called brethren, that you apply to Joseph when he is called father. (*Treatise on Mary's Perpetual Virginity*)

Jerome's teaching on the perpetual virginity of Our Blessed Lady clarified the tradition he had received from the previous century and enabled the doctrine to be firmly rooted in the church. He recognized that we cannot give scientific answers to certain questions. How, for instance, could Mary conceive and give birth to a son and still remain a virgin? Jerome writes, "Let my critics explain to me how Jesus can have entered in through closed doors when He allowed His hands and his side to be handled, and showed that He had bones and flesh, thus proving that He was a true body and no mere phantom of one, and I will explain how the holy Mary can be at once a mother and a virgin."

At the heart of Mary's conception and giving birth is the mystery of the Holy Spirit's creative presence. We are faced with the great mystery of our faith—the mystery of the incarnation of the Son of God. We should expect, therefore, that the Holy Spirit unfolds this mystery in the life of the church. From the earliest times, as we have seen, the conviction of the virgin birth was firmly held in the church. That conviction became a conviction that Mary remained a virgin all her life.

ℰ

St. Augustine of Hippo
A.D. *353-430*

We introduce now the testimony of one of the best known writers of the early church—St. Augustine of Hippo. Augustine was born in Tagaste, North Africa, in A.D. 353 and died as bishop of Hippo in 430. Like Jerome, he was a great defender of Mary's perpetual virginity. In a succinct sentence he stated: "As a Virgin she conceived, as a Virgin she gave birth, and as a Virgin she remained." Like Jerome, Augustine appealed to the resurrection narrative of Jesus passing through closed doors to focus on the mystery of the virginity of Mary:

> Some people get so excited [about Christ's passing through the shut doors], that they pretty nearly risk bringing their prejudices formed from their own reasoning against God's miracles. For they argue thus: If it was a body, if it were flesh and bones, if that which hung on the wood, rose from the sepulchre; how could it enter through closed doors? . . . You have one miracle, you see, in the Lord's conception. Here also one in his birth. A Virgin brought forth Christ, a Virgin she remained. Even then the Lord, before He rose again, was born through closed doors. (*Sermon 247*)

In defending the virginity of Mary, Augustine was also defending the virginity of the church. Mary mirrors the church:

> Let us consider who is this Virgin, so holy, that the Holy Spirit deigned to come to her; so beautiful that God chose her for His spouse; so fruitful that the whole world receives of her bringing forth; so chaste, that she is a Virgin after child birth. See we not under the figure of Mary the type of the Holy Church? For on her too, as you know, the Holy Spirit came down; her too the power of the Most High overshadowed, and from her goes forth Christ, mighty in power. The Church is the immaculate bride, fruitful in child bearing, virgin in chastity. She conceived not from man, but by the Spirit. She gives birth not in sorrow but in joy. She nurtures not with breast of body, but with milk of the Teacher. Hence is she the Spouse of Christ, the mother of the nations, who marvels at seeing herself with child, and rejoices when she has brought forth. (*Sermon 121*)

The Virgin Mary bears and gives birth to Christ, the Son of God, the Head; the church gives birth to the members, the faithful, the Body of Christ. What is true of Mary is true of the church. Both Mary and the church give birth to Christ:

Mary corporally gave birth to the Head of this body, the Church spiritually gives birth to the members of that Head. . . . But she is clearly the spiritual Mother of his members, which we are; because she co-operated by her charity, that the faithful might be born into the Church; and these are the members of the same Head. . . . For the faithful, whether married or virgins consecrated to God, who are of holy living, and charity, and faith unfeigned, are, because they do the will of the Father, spiritually mothers of Christ. (*De Sancta Virginitate*)

Augustine, like the other early fathers, especially Irenaeus, had a keen sense of the parallel between Eve and Mary. The knot of sin was untied in the same way in which it was originally tied. "Because man fell through the female sex, by the female sex was man restored. Because a Virgin had given birth to Christ, a woman announced his resurrection. By a woman death, by a woman life." Sad to say, this very positive view of Augustine on the role of women in our salvation failed to prevail against a more negative appraisal.

৪৯

Jerusalem

We have listened to witnesses from East and West, from Palestine, Egypt, and Turkey, and from Lyons, Milan, and North Africa. In the second, third, fourth, and fifth centuries we find a growing interest in and an emerging devotion to the Virgin Mother of Christ. What were they saying about Mary in Jerusalem, in the city of the crucifixion, the resurrection, and Pentecost? Had you been living in Jerusalem in the fifth century, this is what you would have heard the great preacher Hesychius say:

With good reason does every grateful tongue salute the Virgin and Mother of God, and thus, as far as possible, imitate Gabriel, prince of angels. Thus one says to her: *Hail*, and another: *The Lord is with you: The Lord is of you*, on account of Him who was born of her, and appeared as Our Lord in the flesh of the human race. Again others call her Lamp without orifice that burns of itself, the Ark, wider, longer, and more famous than that of Noe. The prophets therefore vie one with another in their praises of you, O Virgin, and of the God-bearer each one speaks who believed in the mysteries and marvel. Thus one calls you the Rod of Jesse, to image forth the invulnerability and inflexibility of your virginity. Another compares you to the Bush that burned and was not consumed, to typify the flesh of the Only-begotten, and the Virgin Mother of God. For she was on fire, and yet was not consumed, since she brought forth, and at the same time her womb was not opened. One calls her the closed Gate set at the East, that lets in the King with the doors shut at the East because the true light that enlightens every man coming into the world, went forth from the womb, as from a royal bride-chamber. Another called you an enclosed garden and a fountain sealed, even He the Spouse who was born of you, and spoke before in the Canticles. (*Sermon* 5)

Christians in Jerusalem in the fourth and fifth century obviously had a keen interest in Mary. Hesychius could say "with good reason does every faithful tongue salute the Virgin and Mother of God." They had the practice of "saluting" Mary—speaking to her in prayer, praising her by applying to her many of the great religious symbols of the Old Testament such as the Bush, the Ark, and the Rod of Jesse. They had a devotion to Mary. Hesychius inflamed that devotion: "See how great and of what kind is the dignity of the Virgin Mother of God? For the Only-begotten Son of God the world's creator was born as an infant of her, reformed Adam, sanctified Eve, drove out the dragon, and opened Paradise, keeping sure the seal of her womb."

ೞ

St. Cyril of Alexandria
A.D. *370–444*

As our last witness to the faith and teaching of the great early bishops and teachers of the church we will listen to the words of

St. Cyril. During his lifetime a new error concerning Christ was spreading. Some bishops taught that while Mary was the mother of Christ she should not be called the Mother of God. The title *Theotokos,* "God-bearer" or "Mother of God" had been applied to Mary. Objection to this title came from those who divided Christ into two persons, the human person who was born of Mary and the divine person who is forever equal to the Father. Mary was the mother of the human person, the mother of Christ. She was not the mother of the divine person, the mother of God. Cyril wrote:

> That anyone could doubt the right of the holy Virgin to be called the Mother of God fills me with astonishment. Surely she must be the Mother of God if our Lord Jesus Christ is God, and she gave birth to him! Our Lord's disciples may not have used those exact words, but they delivered to us the belief those words enshrine, and this has also been taught us by the holy Father. (*Epistle 1*)

Cyril became the great champion of the divinity of Jesus and the divine motherhood of Mary. When the Council of Ephesus met to respond to this heresy, the teaching of Cyril prevailed. Mary was declared Mother of God. As an example of the preaching and teaching of this great bishop on Mary, and also as an indication of his own devotion and the devotion of the other bishops at the Council of Ephesus, we will listen to his opening homily to the council:

> I see here a joyful company of Christian men met together in ready response to the call of Mary, the holy and ever-virgin Mother of God. The great grief that weighted upon me is changed into joy by your presence, venerable Fathers. Now the beautiful saying of David the psalmist: *How good and pleasant it is for brothers to live together in unity* has come true for us.
>
> Therefore, holy and incomprehensible Trinity, we salute you at whose summons we have come together in this church of Mary, the Mother of God.
>
> Mary, Mother of God, we salute you. Precious vessel; worthy of the whole world's reverence, you are an ever-shining

light, the crown of virginity, the symbol of orthodoxy, an indestructible temple, the place that held him whom no place can contain, mother and virgin. Because of you the holy Gospels could say: Blessed is he who comes in the name of the Lord.

We salute you, for your holy womb has confined him who is beyond all limitation. Because of you the holy Trinity is glorified and adored; the cross is called precious and is venerated throughout the world; the heavens exult; the angels and archangels make merry; demons are put to flight; the devil, that tempter, is thrust down from heaven; the fallen race of man is taken up on high; all creatures possessed by the madness of idolatry have attained knowledge of the truth; believers receive holy baptism; the oil of gladness is poured out; the Church is established throughout the world; pagans are brought to repentance.

What more is there to say? Because of you the light of the only-begotten Son of God has shone upon those who sat in the darkness and in the shadow of death; prophets pronounced the word of God; the apostles preached salvation to the Gentiles; the dead are raised to life, and kings rule by the power of the holy Trinity.

Who can put Mary's high honour into words? She is both mother and virgin. I am overwhelmed by the wonder of this miracle. Of course no one could be prevented from living in the house he had built for himself, yet who would invite mockery by asking his own servant to become his mother?

Behold then the joy of the whole universe. Let the union of God and man in the Son of the virgin Mary fill us with awe and adoration. Let us fear and worship the undivided Trinity as we sing and praise the ever-virgin Mary, the holy temple of God, and of God himself, her Son and spotless Bridegroom. To him be glory for ever. Amen. (*Homily 4*)

This magnificent sermon, one of the greatest sermons in the history of the church, was preached some fifteen hundred years ago. St. Cyril was a faithful witness to the faith that he had received and that he wished to hand on; he gave an eloquent testimony to his own devotion to Mary and to the devotion to the

Mother of God of all those bishops who assembled at the Council of Ephesus. This great defender of the divinity of Jesus was also a great devotee of the mother of Jesus. It was his faith in the divinity of her Son that inspired him to have such love for and confidence in her.

ℱ℈

The Council of Ephesus
A.D. 431

From the testimonies of the great martyrs, saints, and theologians of the first five centuries of the church, we see that each generation fulfilled Mary's prophecy and called her "blessed." As we saw, some heretics denied the humanity of Jesus and others denied his divinity. In answer to each heresy the church invoked the person of Mary and presented her as the great argument in defense of her Son. Her motherhood was the proof of his humanity; her virginity was the proof of his divinity. The Council of Ephesus defended both the divinity of Jesus and the divine motherhood with this declaration: "If anyone does not confess that Emmanuel is truly God and therefore that the blessed Virgin is truly Mother of God (*Theotokos*) for she bore according to the flesh him who is the Word of God, let him be anathema." That declaration of the Catholic faith defined for all time the church's faith in the divinity of Jesus and in Mary's divine motherhood. The Council of Ephesus, building on the teaching of the great saints and teachers of the first four hundred years of the church's existence, laid a sure foundation for the church's understanding of and devotion to Mary the Mother of Jesus. In the next chapter we will see how Marian doctrine developed in the church.

4

Mary in the Doctrine of the Church

℘ T HE GOSPELS TELL US THAT MARY is "the mother of Jesus"; the
church tells us that Mary is "the Mother of God." Mary is
never called "Mother of God" in the Gospels. The citizens of
Nazareth referred to her son as "the son of the carpenter" or "the
son of Joseph." People knew Mary of Nazareth, and they knew
her relationship with Jesus. But none of them knew the hidden
identity of Jesus, namely, that he was the Son of the living God
conceived through the power of the Holy Spirit. This truth,
revealed to Mary at the Annunciation, could only be made
known, as Jesus said to Peter, "by my Father in heaven" (Matt.
16:18). After the resurrection, when the disciples began to believe
and confess that Jesus is the Risen Lord, the deeper meaning of
Mary's motherhood slowly came into focus. She was not just the
mother of the crucified man Jesus; she was the mother of the
Risen Lord Jesus.

℘

The Divine Motherhood

If Mary is the mother of Jesus and if Jesus is the Risen Lord, the
Son of the living God, can we say that Mary is the Mother of
God? For those of us who have been brought up on this faith, it
seems a very logical conclusion. But it was not so for everyone in
the early centuries of the church. Some Christians, as we saw in

the last chapter, denied the true humanity of Jesus, while others denied his divinity. In the fifth century, Nestorius believed that Jesus was indeed the Christ, that he was born of Mary, and that therefore Mary could be called Mother of Christ. She could be called *Christotokos,* the one who bears Christ. She could not, however, in Nestorius's teaching, be called *Theotokos,* the one who bears God, the Mother of God. Nestorius based his distinction on the fact that he attributed two persons to Jesus—the human person in his human nature and a divine person in his divine nature. Mary was the mother of the human nature, the human Jesus, but she was not the mother of the divine person; therefore, she could not be called Mother of God. The church defended the unity of Christ as a person. There is only one person in Christ and that person is divine; that person is the Son of God. Mary is the mother of that person. She is not just the mother of "the human nature." No mother is just the mother of her child's body. She is the mother of the person who grows in her womb, to whom she gives birth, whom she nurses, nurtures, and educates. To clearly establish this vital truth about Jesus and to foster it among the faithful, the Council of Ephesus in 431 decreed: "If anyone does not confess that Emmanuel is truly God and therefore that the blessed Virgin is truly Mother of God (*Theotokos*) for she bore according to the flesh him who is the Word of God, let him be anathema." If Mary is the mother of God then Jesus her Son is the Son of God. The declaration of the Council of Ephesus was reinforced twenty years later by the Council of Constantinople in 451. Mary's divine motherhood thus became a dogma of the church. True faith in Jesus the incarnate Son of God involved faith in the divine maternity of Mary. Pope John Paul II writes:

> The dogma of the divine motherhood of Mary was for the Council of Ephesus and is for the Church like a seal upon the dogma of the Incarnation, in which the Word truly assumes human nature into the unity of his person, without cancelling out that nature. (*Redemptoris mater* 4)

The dogma of our faith that Mary is the Mother of God was not introduced to honor Mary or to put Mary at the center. This dogma was defined to safeguard faith in the incarnation, to defend the divinity of Jesus, and to keep Jesus as the center. This Marian dogma has functioned in the church ever since as the guardian of the doctrine of the incarnation. The doctrine of the divine motherhood is a Christocentric doctrine and clearly safeguards the church's faith in the divinity of Jesus. As Pope John Paul II says,

> In the mystery of Christ Mary is present even "before the creation of the world," as the one whom the Father "has chosen" as Mother of his Son in the Incarnation. And, what is more, together with the Father, the Son has chosen her, entrusting her eternally to the Spirit of holiness. In an entirely special and exceptional way Mary is united to Christ, and similarly she is eternally loved in this "beloved Son," this Son who is of one being with the Father, in whom is concentrated all the "glory of grace." (*Redemptoris mater* 8)

Mary's divine motherhood, predestined by God from all eternity, began in time when she said yes to God. Her consent to the divine request for her cooperation in the mystery of the incarnation was, by God's own decision, necessary for the unfolding in time of the eternal plan of our salvation. The incarnation and the whole mystery of salvation and the church depended on Mary's cooperation as mother. There is, therefore, by God's own choice, a maternal, a Marian, dimension to our salvation. This dimension was very succinctly highlighted by St. Paul in his only reference to Mary in his writings:

> When the appointed time came God sent his Son, born of a woman, born a subject of the Law, to redeem the subjects of the Law and to enable us to be adopted as sons. The proof that you are sons is that God sent the Spirit of his Son into our hearts, the Spirit that cries "Abba, Father!" (Gal. 4:4-6)

Commenting on this verse Pope John Paul II says that these words "celebrate together the love of the Father, the mission of the Son, the gift of the Spirit, the role of the woman from whom the Redeemer was born, and our own divine filiation, in the mystery of the 'fullness of time'" (*Redemptoris mater* 1). Paul, in his only reference to Mary, places her in the context of the fulfillment of the trinitarian plan of salvation. Through Mary's willing cooperation the plan of the Holy Trinity for the human race took flesh and blood. It is impossible, therefore, to consider God's plan for our salvation without acknowledging Mary's maternal role and the Marian dimension of the mystery of our redemption. As Leonardo Boff said,

> Mary is actually the pivotal point of all salvation history, then, both from the side of God and the side of humanity. On her that twofold history is supported and revolves. We cannot bypass Mary's essential meaning. Those who do so empty Christianity of its historicity. It is impossible to accept the incarnate God without accepting Mary who gave God human flesh![1]

Mary's motherhood of Jesus, now defined in the church as her "divine motherhood," was so necessary for our salvation that without it Jesus would not have been truly human. "There is only one God and there is only one mediator between God and mankind, himself a human being, Christ Jesus, who sacrificed himself as a ransom for all" (1 Tim. 2:4). It is in his humanity that Jesus becomes our unique mediator. And Jesus receives his human nature from his mother. The more we stress the uniqueness of Jesus as our one mediator with the Father, the clearer we focus on Mary's maternal contribution to the divine plan. Without Mary there would be no Jesus; without Jesus there would be no mediator between God and us. As the Second Vatican Council said, "The Father of mercies willed that the Incarnation should be preceded by the assent on the part of the predestined mother, so that just as a woman had a share in bringing about death, so also a woman should contribute to life" (*Lumen Gentium* 56).

Mary freely chose her divine motherhood; her consent was a faith-inspired, fully responsible human act; God's grace, active within her freedom, enabled her to respond with the inspired words, "Let it be done unto me according to your word" (Luke 1:38).

---

 formulaire

Mother of the Redeemer

Mary freely consented to be the mother not just of the "baby Jesus" but of Jesus the Redeemer. The angel told her in detail who her son would be: "He will be great and will be called the Son of the Most High. The Lord God will give him the throne of his ancestor David; he will rule over the House of Jacob forever and his reign will have no end" (Luke 1:32–34). Mary knew the promises that had been made to her people; she knew the prophecies; she did not know the full implications of how her Son's reign would last forever. But she knew, through the light of faith, that her Son was the Messiah, the promised Redeemer. And she said yes to mothering the Redeemer of the human race. Her consent to the mothering of the Messiah was her consent to our salvation, a consent that would take her from Nazareth to Bethlehem, and finally to Jerusalem and Calvary. She remained faithful to the consent she gave to the angel even when Jesus was dying on the cross.

Mary's maternal consent given at Nazareth was confirmed on Calvary as she, in the words of the council, "associated herself with his sacrifice in her mother's heart" (*Lumen Gentium* 57). Hence, we say that Mary cooperated not just with the birth of Jesus but also with his redemptive death. She is, therefore, truly the Mother of the Redeemer. As the Vatican Council said,

> She conceived, brought forth, and nourished Christ, she presented him to the Father in the temple, shared her Son's sufferings as he died on the cross. Thus, in a wholly singular way she co-operated by her obedience, faith, hope and burning charity in the work of the Savior in restoring supernatural life to souls. For this reason she is a mother to us in the order of grace. (*Lumen Gentium* 61)

Mary's cooperation with her Son in the work of our redemption was entirely his gift to her; his grace in her enabled her to welcome his redeeming death and to offer him in love to the Father.

ℬ

Mother of the Redeemed

Mary is the mother of the whole Christ. As St. Paul says, "Now Christ's body is yourselves, each of you with a part to play in the whole" (1 Cor. 12:27). As Mother of "the whole Christ," Mary is the spiritual mother of each member of Christ. She is the Mother of the Church. Again according to Vatican II,

> This motherhood of Mary in the order of grace continues without interruption from the consent which she loyally gave at the Annunciation and which she sustained without wavering beneath the cross, until the eternal fulfillment of all the elect. Taken up into heaven she did not lay aside this saving office but by her manifold intercession continues to bring us the gifts of eternal salvation. By her motherly love she cares for her Son's sisters and brothers who still journey on earth surrounded by dangers and difficulties, until they are led into their blessed home. Therefore the Blessed Virgin is invoked in the Church under the titles of Advocate, Helper, Benefactress, and Mediatrix. This, however, is understood in such a way that it neither takes away anything from, nor adds anything to the dignity and efficacy of Christ the one Mediator. (*Lumen Gentium* 62)

That Jesus Christ, the Son of Mary, is our one and only mediator with God the Father is the center of our faith. Mary is not the mediator. But Mary is the Mother. She is the Mother of Christ, the whole Christ, head and members. That is why we call her not just Mother of Christ but Our Mother. That too is why we call Jesus our brother. He is our brother because by his gift on the cross Mary is our mother. How could we call Jesus our brother if we refused to call Mary our mother? And if Mary is our mother "in the order of grace," how could we refuse to acknowledge or celebrate her motherhood?

৯৯

Mary as the Image
or Model of the Church

Mary, in her divine motherhood, has been seen from earliest times as the image, type, or model of the church. The Second Vatican Council reaffirmed this understanding:

> By reason of the gift and role of her divine motherhood, by which she is united with her Son, the Redeemer, and with her unique graces and functions, the Blessed Virgin is also intimately united to the church. As St. Ambrose taught, the Mother of God is a type of the church in the order of faith, charity, and perfect union with Christ. For in the mystery of the church, which is itself rightly called mother and virgin, the Blessed Virgin stands out in eminent and singular fashion as exemplar both of virgin and mother to her Son, the Redeemer, and with his singular graces and offices. By these, the Blessed Virgin is also intimately united with the Church: the Mother of God is a figure of the Church in the matter of faith, charity and perfect union with Christ. (*Lumen Gentium* 63)

Just as Mary became the mother of Christ, through believing the Word of God and the overshadowing of the Holy Spirit, so the church becomes the mother of the Mystical Body of Christ: "accepting with fidelity the Word of God, by her preaching and by baptism she brings forth new and immortal children conceived of the Holy Spirit and born of God" (*Lumen Gentium* 64). The church sees in Mary's divine motherhood all that she is called to be and do. As Pope John Paul II says,

> It can be said that from Mary the Church also learns her own motherhood: she recognizes the maternal dimension of her

vocation, which is essentially bound to her sacramental nature, "in contemplating Mary's mysterious sanctity, imitating her charity and faithfully fulfilling the Father's will." If the church is the sign and instrument of intimate union with God, she is so by reason of her motherhood, because receiving life from the Spirit, she "generates" sons and daughters of the human race. For just as Mary is at the service of the mystery of the Incarnation, so the Church is always at the service of the mystery of adoption to sonship through grace. (*Redemptoris mater* 43)

Mary's motherhood is not confined to the mothering of Jesus. It extends, through Christ's will, to the church. Mary is the Mother of the Church. The church's own motherhood with regard to the faithful is patterned on Mary's motherhood of Jesus. The church shares with Mary the same vocation, namely, giving birth to Christ in the world. Mary gave birth to the physical body of Christ; the church gives birth to the Mystical Body of Christ. The church sees in Mary the perfect mirror of herself. What God has done in Mary he is now doing in the church. Therefore, the church can never reflect on herself and on her mission in the world without remembering Mary and her mission in the world. There is a Marian dimension in the church because there is a Marian dimension in Christ. In a letter to me, the great moral theologian Bernard Häring wrote, "My love of Mary and my love of the Church are intertwined. It brings into my deepest feeling the absolute balance between the fatherly and the motherly love of God, who is both our Father and our Mother." No one expressed this truth better than Isaac of Stella in his celebrated passage:

By their divine regeneration, Christians are one with him [Christ]. The one Christ, the unique and whole Christ, is the head and the members. He is the only-begotten Son, in heaven, of a unique God, and on earth, of a unique mother; at the same time many sons and one only Son. As the head and the members are only one Son, yet, at the same time, being

many sons, so Mary and the Church are at once one mother
and several, one virgin and several. The one and the other are
mothers, the one and the other are virgins; the one and the
other conceive of the same Spirit, without concupiscence; the
one and the other bring forth progeny to the Father, without
sin. . . . The one and the other are the mother of Christ, but
neither of the two have brought him forth entirely. That is
why in the divinely inspired Scriptures, what is said of the
Church virgin-mother in the collective sense (*universaliter*) is
valid of Mary in the individual sense (*singulariter*) and that
which is said specifically (*specialiter*) of Mary virgin-mother,
one may with good reason understand it in a general manner
(*generaliter*) of the Church virgin-mother; and when a text has
been composed on the subject of the one or the other, one
may understand it very well of the one or the other. Moreover,
each believing soul may be considered, under a certain relationship, as spouse of the Word of God, mother of the Christ,
his daughter, his sister, virgin and at the same time fecund.
Since, then, that which is said in the collective sense (*universaliter*) for the Church, and specifically (*specialiter*) for Mary, is
valid also in the individual sense (*singulariter*) for each believing soul. That is what the very Wisdom of God, which is the
Word of the Father, teaches us.[2]

℘ঌ

Virgin Mother

The virginal conception of Jesus is clearly witnessed to by the
Gospels according to Matthew and Luke, and some would argue
also by the Gospel according to John. St. Matthew makes it very
clear that Joseph is not the father of Jesus. To highlight this fact
Matthew introduces the genealogy of Jesus naming the father of
each ancestor: Abraham was the father of Isaac, Isaac the father of
Jacob, Jacob the father of Judah, and so on, until we arrive at
another Jacob, who was "the father of Joseph the husband of

Mary; of her was born Jesus who is called Christ" (Matt. 1:16). In his genealogy Matthew mentions thirty-six men who were the fathers of Jesus' ancestors. But, when he comes to speak of Jesus' own birth he dramatically changes the sequence and says "Joseph was the husband of Mary; of her was born Jesus who is called Christ." And Matthew tells us how Jesus was conceived. The angel told Joseph "she has conceived what is in her by the Holy Spirit" (Matt. 1:21). Mary herself raises the issue of her virginity in Luke's Gospel when she says to the angel, "But how can this come about, since I am a virgin." The angel gave her the explanation: "The Holy Spirit will come upon you and the power of the Most High will cover you with its shadow" (Luke 1:34–35). Luke also makes it clear that Mary's townsfolk considered Joseph to be the father of her son: "being the son, as it was thought, of Joseph" (3:23). Some scholars argue that when St. John speaks of "those who believed in his name, who were born not from human stock or human desire or human will but from God himself" (John 1:13), he is referring to the virginal conception of Jesus.

These references in the Gospels to the virginal conception of Jesus were understood in the earliest tradition of the church as belonging the greater mystery of the person of Jesus, to the incarnation. St. Ignatius of Antioch wrote:

> Now the virginity of Mary was hidden from the prince of this world, as was her offspring and the death of the Lord: three mysteries loudly shouted out, which, however, were wrought in silence and, yet, have been revealed to us.[3]

Ignatius, teaching the faith before the final books of the New Testament were written, states that the "virginity of Mary" has been revealed to us. It belongs to revelation; it hasn't been scientifically demonstrated. God is saying something to us about Jesus in revealing to us his virginal conception. The church has understood clearly that this revelation concerns the very person of Jesus, concerns the fact that he is the preexisting Son of God. His was a miraculous conception without human intercourse.

Raymond Brown wrote that "the totality of the scientifically con-trollable evidence leaves an unresolved problem."[4] Yet from the very early Christian writings we see how the church understood the Gospels. Long before Mary received the title Mother of God she had the title Virgin. The very earliest creeds of the church profess "Jesus Christ, born of the Virgin Mary." In the Apostles' Creed we say, "And in Jesus Christ, his only Son, Our Lord, who was conceived by the Holy Spirit and born of the Virgin Mary."

The doctrine of the virgin birth concerns the person of Jesus and should not be interpreted as a negative judgment on human sexuality. In the world in which Mary grew up, virginity was not a sign of any special moral or spiritual status. It was a sign of great weakness, the equivalent of sterility. Indeed, when the Bible wishes to describe the misery of the people in one of their dark-est hours, the prophets compared them to a virgin: "Listen to this oracle I speak against you, it is a dirge, House of Israel: She has fallen down, never to rise again, the virgin Israel" (Amos 5:1-2). Virginity was not a noble or sought-after state; it was a state of human weakness, a state of barrenness. Ivone Gebara and Maria Clara Bingemer write: "The 'impotence' of Mary's virgin body is a figure of humankind's poverty when it comes to achieving its own salvation without God's grace."[5] In choosing Mary the Virgin, God chooses the poor, the lowly, the one whom society rejects. There was no expectation among the Jews that the Messiah would be born of a virgin. The Gospel accounts of the virginal conception of Jesus could not, then, have been condi-tioned by any messianic expectation at the time. Much less could the pagan mythology of the birth of demigods from intercourse between pagan gods and women on earth have influenced the writers of the Gospels. Such mythology was totally repugnant to the faith of the Jews. The fact that the Gospels include the story of the virginal conception of Jesus can only be explained by the faith of the writers and the faith of the communities for which they wrote the Gospels. This was a revealed truth about Jesus' human origin.

Some writers today argue that Jesus was the fruit of a normal marriage relationship between Mary and Joseph but that he was truly the Son of God. Could Jesus, they ask, be truly human if he was not conceived like any other human being? They overlook the fact that Adam, the father of us all, was not conceived like every other human being. Adam was created directly by God. Jacques Bur is correct when he writes: "A child born of a relationship of interpersonal love between a human father and a human mother is a human person. To have become incarnate, God would have had to have hindered this human personalization, putting the person of his own divine Son in this small human being born of the will of a man and a woman."[6] A child born of a human couple is a human person, and that person can only become the Son of God by adoption. As Bur says, "The history of heresies from the Ebionites in the first century to the Modernists in the twentieth shows that the opponents of the virginal conception were also, for the most part, opponents of the divinity of Jesus, whom they recognised as Son of God by adoption."[7] The church throughout the centuries has defended the virginity of Mary because it always defends the divinity of Mary's Son. The virgin birth is the sign of that divinity. It is the sign that in Jesus there is a new beginning, a new Adam, a fresh start for the human race. And all this comes from God's initiative.

Some object that the emphasis on the virgin birth is demeaning of human sexuality. The implication is, they say, that it is more appropriate for Jesus to be conceived virginally than to be conceived through normal marital intercourse. They also point out that with the emergence of monasticism in the church the monks, who were celibate ascetics, had a negative attitude to marriage and extolled the state of virginity to justify their own way of life. It is not, however, sexuality but fatherhood that is in question. Mary's virginity should not be read as God's preference for the unmarried state. Marriage, as St. Paul tells us, is the sign of the union of Christ and the church. Within the church marriage has the dignity of a sacrament. The church couldn't bestow on the state of marriage a greater dignity than that. By affirming, however, the virginity of Mary, the human origin of Jesus the Son of God, the church is at the same time affirming his divine origin. That is the significance of Mary's virginity. It is the sign of God's sovereign grace and initiative in our salvation. The British Methodist–Roman Catholic Committee expressed this well:

> Mary's virginal conception of Jesus was especially fitting in that it highlights God's gracious act of bringing about the new creation in Christ. Like the first creation, the new creation begun in Jesus is entirely the work of God. Jesus is literally a "Godsend." "In the beginning," Adam (humanity's beginning) is pictured as being created by the power of the Spirit from barren soil (Gen 2:6); in the new beginning, the humanity of Christ, the Second Adam, is created from the virginity of Mary by the same overshadowing power of the Spirit of Life. Neither the first nor the second Adam were any less human as a consequence of their unique way of coming to be.[8]

The church also believes and teaches that in the act of giving birth Mary remained a virgin. In consenting to become the mother of Jesus in her virginal state, Mary consecrated her virginity to God. That was all she had to offer to God. Her state of virginity—by human standards, barrenness—became the fertile ground for the incarnation. Through that gift of her virginal being to God she became, through the overshadowing of the Holy Spirit, the mother of Jesus. That gift of herself to God was a consecration of her whole being to the service of her Son. In coming to birth, Jesus consecrated her womb and sanctified her virginity. The Second Vatican Council speaks of "the firstborn son who did not diminish his mother's virginal integrity but sanctified it" (*Lumen Gentium* 57). Whether the actual physical birth of Jesus was painless or even miraculous we do not know. All the Gospel tells us is that Mary, "gave birth to a son, her first-born. She wrapped him in swaddling clothes, and laid him a manger because there was no room for them in the living-space" (Luke 2:7).

꽃

Ever Virgin

God's eternal plan for the coming of his Son into the world
involved not just the choice of Mary as the mother of Jesus but
also the choice of Joseph as the husband of Mary and legal father
of Jesus. Scripture doesn't give us details about the marriage of
Mary and Joseph, but from the earliest times the church held the
conviction that they lived their marriage without a normal sexual
relationship. This does not mean that Mary lived in a loveless
marriage. It was revealed to Joseph her husband that she had conceived through the power of the Holy Spirit—hence, perhaps, his
fear of "taking Mary as his wife." He recognized that Mary
belonged to God in a most unique way. When God's word freed
him from that fear, he took Mary as his wife and we see him as
the protective and caring provider in the background. Through
their love for one another, through the deep friendship and inti-
macy they shared, they provided a warm, human environment, a
home for the Holy Family in which Jesus could be nurtured and
develop as a whole and healthy person. Mary bore no children to
Joseph. The only early father of the church to dispute this was
Tertullian. Those who are referred to as the brothers and sisters
of the Lord are his first cousins, children of Joseph by a previous
marriage, or children of Joseph's sister. This interpretation is dis-
puted today, and many Protestant Scripture commentators argue
that Joseph and Mary had children together. Biblical scholarship
alone cannot give a definitive answer to all the questions that
can be raised. In 1973, the bishops of the United States stated:

> The teaching about Mary's lifelong virginity is an example of
> the Church's growth in understanding of Christian doctrine.
> In its ordinary teaching, reflected in catechesis and liturgy, as
> well as in more formal pronouncements, the Church has here

recognized as an aspect of "public revelation" a belief not
clearly demonstrable from the Scriptures. (*Behold Your Mother*
50)

At the end of all the theological and scriptural debates about the
virginity of Mary, Catholic faith rests not on the opinion of
experts but on the teaching of the church. As the bishops of the
United States said, "What is normative in the matter of the Virgin
birth is the teaching of the Church. The Bible is read rightly in
the Church, whose interpretation is guided by the Holy Spirit"
(*Behold Your Mother* 43). Throughout the history of the church,
belief in Mary's perpetual virginity has been strong and constant. The church holds that this belief has developed through
the guidance of the Holy Spirit. That is why the church proposes
this doctrine of our faith. We believe that Jesus was born of the
Virgin Mary, and we believe that Mary remained a virgin.

₰

The Immaculate Conception

At a very early age I had to memorize this prayer: "O Mary conceived without sin, pray for us who have recourse to thee." I had
no idea what it meant. I had no idea at all what "conceived"
meant. Later on I came to treasure this prayer because it spoke to
me about original innocence. Original sin, the "fall of our first
parents," was represented by Adam and Eve; original innocence
was represented by the Virgin Mary. Mary owed her "original
innocence," her state of holiness, her "unfallen state," to the
merits of Jesus Christ her Son. Through the merits of Jesus,
through his work of redemption, his mother was preserved free
from sin so that from the very first moment of her existence she
was always a friend of God. At no time in her existence was she
alienated from God. As a young boy, I was introduced to this
understanding of Mary. All Catholics believed this about Our
Lady and it always made sense to me. God surely wouldn't choose

someone who was an enemy, in whose heart the Holy Spirit had not poured out the love of God, to be the mother of the Son of God. But where did we get this understanding of Our Lady from?

There is no mention of the "Immaculate Conception" of Mary in the Scriptures. The first time Mary is mentioned is when she was about to conceive her own son. We are told that the angel Gabriel called her by the name *kecharitōmenē*, "full of grace" or "most highly favored one." Jacques Bur writes:

> *kecharitōmenē* does not refer literally to the fullness of sancti-fying grace given to Mary at the time of her conception, but to the favour done to her of being mother of the Lord. How-ever, the personal holiness of Mary is certainly implied in this term which is presented as a proper name given to Mary, as being inherent in the very grace of her motherhood.[9]

At the moment of the Annunciation, God saw Mary as sinless. He was saying that because she was "full of grace" she was now pre-pared to undertake a work of grace, the special mission that he was giving to her. Through the power of the Holy Spirit she was ready to respond freely to his invitation and become the mother of Jesus Christ his Son. Her whole life, her whole state of being "full of grace" made her a fit dwelling for the Son of God. "The grace of motherhood implies in Mary a state of supernatural grace which makes her fully worthy to receive the saviour in her womb."[10]

When and how did Mary become "full of grace"? As the church began to ponder these questions, it began to discern the deeper mystery of the Immaculate Conception. During the early centuries of the church, as we saw in chapter 3, whenever there was an error about the person of Jesus, denying his humanity or denying his divinity, the church responded by teaching that Mary is truly the mother of God and that she conceived Jesus vir-ginally. When the theological questions moved away from the person of Jesus to his work of redemption, other issues emerged. Christ redeemed us from the state of original sin. What is this state? How does it happen that we come to be "born in the state of original sin"? And if all human beings are born in the state of original sin, was Mary, the Mother of God, born in this state? Long before there was any reflection on the nature of original sin, there was a deeply held conviction that Mary was all holy, that she did not commit any personal sin. The Eastern churches were never too concerned about defining what they meant by original sin. But the Western church, especially under the influence of St. Augustine, became very concerned with the nature of this original sin and with its transmission. For Augustine, original sin is transmitted from parents to children through sexual intercourse. Jesus was conceived through the power of the Holy Spirit, without sexual intercourse, so there was never any question about his having contacted original sin. But since Mary was conceived in the normal way, she must have had original sin. Augustine's identification of sexual intercourse as the means through which original sin was transmitted posed many theological difficulties. But, while theologians were pondering this problem, the faithful were joyfully celebrating the sinlessness of Mary. She was "Holy Mary," a great inspiration and a great advocate. As Gebara and Bingemer write:

> From the very beginning of the church, popular faith has played an important role in establishing what would subsequently become the dogma of the immaculate conception. As far back as the second century, the apocryphal Gospel of James included a story from popular circles about the conception of Mary by Anne, her mother, already advanced in years, without the intervention of man. Although there are no statements about this in the councils of the first centuries, many of the Church's Fathers are unending in their praise of Mary and call her most holy. In his controversy with the Pelagians Augustine goes so far as to say that "piety demands that we recognise Mary as without sin" and "for the sake of the Lord's honour" Mary in no way "comes under consideration with regard to sin." In the next few centuries one can see a division between popular faith—which stood on the side of the immaculate conception—and a portion of more learned theology which stood opposed.[11]

From earliest times, then, Mary was accepted in the church as the sinless, holy mother of God. Bur writes:

> Without doubt some Greek Fathers—Origen, John Chrystostom and Cyril of Alexandria—accepted that Mary could have known some shortcomings of vanity at the time of the miracle of Cana, or of faith, at the foot of the cross. In contrast the Latin Fathers resolutely argued for the absence of all sin in Mary. And St. Thomas Aquinas, who did not accept the Immaculate Conception, affirmed without beating around the bush: "The Blessed Virgin Mary received such full intensity of grace that it brought her right next to the author of grace in order to receive him, who has the full intensity of grace in himself."[12]

Mary was the sinless mother of Jesus. When did she become sinless? How did she become sinless? Popular devotion to the Mother of God, contemplation of "the great things God had done in her" in choosing her to be the mother of Jesus, and prayerful trust in her powerful intercession led the faithful to the conviction of her Immaculate Conception long before the theologians had found all the answers to the problems this belief raised. The problems were real. Mary, like the rest of the children of Adam, needed salvation. Christ had to be her Savior. If she was conceived without sin how could she have been saved by Christ? How could she be "freed from sin" by Christ if she had never been "bound by sin"? Even great theologians like St. Bernard and St. Thomas Aquinas, who had such deep devotion to Mary and who celebrated her great holiness, did not find satisfactory answers to these questions. The Franciscan Duns Scotus, who died in the year 1308, saw the way through the difficulties.

> He developed the idea of preservative redemption as being a more perfect one: to have been preserved free from original sin was a greater grace than to be set free from sin. Scotus pointed out that not only is prevention better than cure, but that cure aspires to prevention. He considered original sin as a lack, a privation in our human nature, and believed that this privation did not exist in Mary because a redemption that pre-

serves from sin is more perfect than one that frees from sin. The very purpose of Christ's coming was to bring us the fullness of life. In Mary's case this redemption was anticipatory. The debate did not end with Scotus, but his position solved the principal Christological objection.[13]

When did Mary experience this "preservative redemption"? Pope John Paul II begins his encyclical letter *The Mother of the Redeemer* (*Redemptoris mater*) by reflecting on the eternal plan of God as outlined by St. Paul: "Thus he [God] chose us in Christ before the world was made to be holy and faultless before him in love, marking us out for himself beforehand, to be his adopted sons through Jesus Christ" (Eph. 1:4). In God's eternal plan for the incarnation of his Son, Mary was already chosen. She would appear in the history of our human race at a special time, which St. Paul calls "the fullness of time," the "appointed time" (Gal. 4:4). Mary, chosen from all eternity to be the mother of Jesus and prepared by grace for this unique motherhood, is born when the time appointed by God for our salvation arrives. As John Macquarrie, a theologian of the Anglican Communion, writes:

> God proposed to bring the human race not only into existence but into a loving communion with himself. He purposed to do this (so it is claimed in the Christian revelation) by himself assuming humanity and tabernacling with his people. He must then also have purposed to bring the human race to that moment in its history when it had been so cleared of sin and sanctified by grace that it would be ready to receive the gift of the incarnate divine life. That moment in the history of mankind was Mary.[14]

In the fullness of time, according to God's own choice, Mary is born free from all sin so that the Son of God can take flesh in her womb. And such was God's grace of redemption in Mary that she was, from the first moment of her existence, the sinless and beloved daughter of God. As Scotus said, Mary experienced preservative redemption, which prevented original sin from touching her existence, and not restorative redemption, which frees us from sin.

How could Mary have been freed from original sin through the merits of Christ before he was born? We have to look at God's perspective, not our own, when we try to discuss this question. In God's sight there is neither yesterday nor tomorrow. There is only now, the eternal present. God doesn't have to wait for something to happen before he knows all about it. God didn't have to wait for Jesus to die before he knew that we are reconciled through his death and resurrection. The difference between Mary and us, in the plan of salvation, is that for the sake of his Son, God filled her with the grace of redemption before the historical event of the death of Jesus. That is the faith of the church which Pope Pius IX solemnly defined on 8 December 1854: "We declare . . . that the Most Blessed Virgin Mary in the first moment of her conception was, by the unique grace and privilege of God, in view of the merits of Jesus Christ the Savior of the human race, preserved intact from all stain of original sin" (*Ineffabilis Deus*).

Before Pope Pius IX defined the doctrine of Mary's Immaculate Conception he consulted all the bishops of the Catholic Church. Only four or five bishops in the whole Catholic Church thought that the doctrine could not be defined. The doctrine was universally believed in the church. The doctrine of Mary's Immaculate Conception is not true because it has been defined. Rather, it was defined because it is true.

Since 1854 the doctrine of the Immaculate Conception of Our Blessed Lady has been an integral and obligatory part of Catholic faith. The manner of its proclamation by Pope Pius IX has posed great problems for the Anglican and Protestant churches as well as for the Orthodox churches in the East. But many Protestants, prescinding from the actual proclamation of the dogma and reflecting on the substance of the doctrine, now feel much more comfortable with this teaching on Mary. John de Satge, an evangelical theologian, in his greatly acclaimed book *Mary and the Christian Gospel,* wrote:

> The Immaculate Conception of Mary gives the clue to understanding her particular place among her Son's people. She is the first Christian, the first of the redeemed; the first of our

> flawed human race to have received the fullness of redemption. From first to last–in Catholic dogma, from Immaculate Conception to Assumption–she was a human being transformed by the grace of God into what in the divine purpose she was intended to be.[15]

The church which declares Mary immaculate, all holy, and sinless, also gives her the title Refuge of Sinners. Instead of removing her from the terrestrial plane of poor sinners, the doctrine of the Immaculate Conception has filled the church with greater confidence in Mary's maternal love and understanding of all our weaknesses. Mary, our perfectly redeemed mother, has a mother's love and care of each of her children as we stumble and fall on our pilgrimage in this life. Because Mary is pure, holy, and undefiled, we can pray with total confidence, "O Mary conceived without sin, pray for us who have recourse to thee."

The Assumption

Scripture is silent about the death of Mary. We don't know where or when or how she died. There is no mention of her Assumption into heaven in the writings of the first five centuries. Yet within the faith of the church there developed the conviction that Mary was assumed body and soul into heaven. From the sixth century onward this conviction of faith was strong in the universal church, in both East and West. Michael O'Carroll writes:

> The liturgy was to play a part in the development of doctrine. The origins of the feast are far from clear. The starting-point was Jerusalem. There was a hesitancy and variation even in the name used for the feast as time passed. Dormition, Passing, Assumption. Certain facts are fixed, but evidence from lectionaries and from homiletics has still to be sifted. The feast of the Dormition was decreed for Constantinople on the 15 August by emperor Maurice in 600; about fifty years later it

was introduced in Rome and mentioned in a papal decree of Sergius (687–701) who fixed a procession for the feast.[16]

The silence of the first five centuries on what happened to Mary after her death was broken from the sixth century onward with the liturgical celebration of her Assumption. Her glorious Assumption into heaven became universally believed in the church, East and West, and on 1 November 1950 it was proclaimed a dogma of the Catholic faith by Pope Pius XII.

Many theological questions are raised by the doctrine of the Assumption. Since the doctrine is not explicitly found in the Scriptures, and since there is a silence during the first five centuries, how could the church believe in such a doctrine? What legitimacy does a tradition that does not go back to the earliest days of the church have? Jacques Bur comments:

> The essential question here is that of the authority of tradition in the Church. It is this that still divides Protestants and Catholics today. Christ did not entrust his Gospel to a book which he wrote, but charged his Church to hand it down, promising the Church the presence of the Holy Spirit.[17]

Within the worship and prayer of the Catholic Church, belief in the Assumption of the Mother of Jesus dawned, developed, and became universal. The faith of the people, the *consensus fidelium* is, in itself, a source of the faith. The Second Vatican Council said:

> The whole body of the faithful who have an anointing that comes from the holy one (cf. 1 Jn 2:20 and 27) cannot be mistaken in matters of belief. It shows this characteristic through the entire people's supernatural appreciation of the faith, when "from the bishops to the least of the faithful" it manifests a universal consensus in matters of faith and morals. By this sense of faith, aroused and sustained by the Spirit of truth, the People of God, guided by the sacred magisterium which it faithfully obeys, receives not the word of human beings, but truly the word of God (cf. 1 Thess 2:13), "the faith once for all delivered to the saints" (cf. Jude 3). (*Lumen Gentium,* 12)

The church believes that her faith in the Assumption of Our Lady was "aroused and sustained by the Spirit of truth." As the church pondered the mystery of Mary's divine motherhood, it began to see that the sinless mother of Jesus the Risen Lord was already sharing in his victory over sin and death. Christ's human, risen, and glorified body was born of Mary. He was flesh of her flesh. Could Christ allow the body of his sinless mother, who gave birth to his own victorious and risen body, to lie in the corruption of the grave? Would Christ, who will share his resurrection with all his brothers and sisters at the end of time, not anticipate this general resurrection and receive his mother, body and soul, into heaven? Would not the "preservative redemption" that kept her free from original sin keep her free from the corruption and decay that are the result of sin? And what about Jesus' own filial sentiments, his own love of and honor for his mother? Pope Pius XII appeals to this filial love of Jesus when he writes:

> It seems impossible to think of her, the one who conceived Christ, brought him forth, nursed him with her milk, held him in her arms, and clasped him in her breast, as being apart from him in body, even though not in soul, after this earthly life. Since the Redeemer is the Son of Mary, he could not do otherwise, as the perfect observer of God's law, than to honor, not only his eternal Father, but also his most beloved Mother. And since it was within his power to grant this great honor, to preserve her from the corruption of the tomb, we must believe that he really acted in this way. (Apostolic Constitution *Munificentissimus Deus*)

Mary's divine motherhood, which is clearly revealed in the Scriptures, is the ultimate ground for believing in both her Immaculate Conception and her Assumption. The universal belief of the Catholic Church has been that because she is the Mother of God, Christ already shares with her, body and soul, his risen glory. Christ ascended, through his own power as Son of God, into glory; Mary was assumed by the power of Christ her

Son into glory. Her Assumption is an anticipation of the general resurrection, when we will all be raised from the dead. As Our Blessed Lady is now, so we will be. In the words of the Second Vatican Council:

> In the meantime the Mother of Jesus in the glory which she possesses in body and soul in heaven is the image and the beginning of the Church as it is to be perfected in the world to come. Likewise she shines forth on earth, until the day of the Lord shall come (cf. 2 Pet. 3:10), as a sign of certain hope and comfort to the pilgrim People of God. (*Lumen Gentium* 68)

As Mary is now, the Church will be in the future. Mary, our sister, sharing fully in our human nature, born of human parents, just as we were, nourished and brought up in a human family, has now reached the perfect fulfillment of her being. Her death has been transformed in the victory of her Assumption. She is the perfectly fulfilled human being, the model or mirror of what we will become.

As Mother of Christ, Mary was assumed into heaven, where she continues to be Christ's mother and also our mother. Bur writes:

> If the dogma of the Assumption of Mary is first of all associated with that of her divine motherhood, it would also seem to be closely associated with the traditional doctrine of Mary's spiritual motherhood of all human beings. Would Mary today be totally our mother if for us she was only a saint glorified in her body but still waiting for bodily glorification? Could Mary personally and directly know each one of us as her child if she had not already attained the glory of the resurrection?[18]

Because Mary in body and soul, in her whole person, is now with Christ in heaven, she can relate to each of her children on earth in an individual and personal way. In the new creation, where God is all in all, Mary can now have a personal relationship with all the members of Christ's body on earth, with the church. The Second Vatican Council said, "Taken up to heaven she did not lay aside this saving office but by her manifold intercession continues to procure for us the gifts of eternal salvation. By her motherly love she cares for her Son's sisters and brothers who still journey on earth surrounded by dangers and difficulties, until they are led to their blessed home" (*Lumen Gentium* 62). Because of her glorious Assumption, her complete transformation in Christ, Mary is now present as mother to each of us in the mystery of Christ, the mystery of the church.

After the definition of the Immaculate Conception, it seemed only a matter of time before the doctrine of the Assumption would be defined. It took almost a hundred years, but that is a short time in the life of the church. Pope Pius XII had consulted the church widely on the possibility of defining the doctrine as a dogma of faith. He put this question to all the bishops of the Catholic Church: "In your wisdom and prudence, do you think that the bodily assumption of the blessed Virgin Mary could be proposed and defined as a dogma of the faith, and do you, your clergy and your faithful want this?" Over 98 percent of the replies that came into the Vatican were affirmative. Only six bishops expressed doubts about the possibility of the pope being able to define this doctrine as a dogma of faith. Convinced by this clear evidence of the universality of this belief in the Assumption in the Catholic Church, Pope Pius XII defined the doctrine with these words:

> For which reason, after we have poured forth prayers of supplication again and again to God, and have invoked the light of the Spirit of Truth, for the glory of Almighty God who has lavished his special affection upon the Virgin Mary, for the honour of her Son, the immortal King of the Ages and the Victor over sin and death, for the increase of the glory of that same august Mother, and for the joy and exultation of the entire Church; by the authority of our Lord Jesus Christ, of the Blessed Apostles Peter and Paul, and by our own authority, we pronounce, declare, and define it to be a divinely revealed dogma that the Immaculate Mother of God, the ever Virgin

Mary, having completed the course of her earthly life, was assumed body and soul into heavenly glory. (*Munificentissimus Deus* 44)

ℱ

Mary's Intercession

St. Teresa of Avila, a doctor of the church, wrote:

It is clear to me that if we wish to please God and to receive graces in abundance from him, it is God's will that these graces should come to us through the hands of Christ in his most holy humanity, that humanity in which his Majesty has proclaimed that he is well pleased. Apart from the fact that God himself has told me this, time and time again I have noticed it in my own experience; I say it again, I have seen with my own eyes that it is by this door that we must enter if we wish his Supreme Majesty to reveal to us great and hidden mysteries. (Office of Readings, 15 October)

St. Teresa has clearly stated the church's teaching on Christ as the source of all our graces. All the graces of our salvation come to us through Christ.

Jesus Christ in his sacred humanity is our one Mediator with the Father. But his birth as our Redeemer was due to the consent and cooperation of Mary, his mother. Her maternal cooperation with her Son didn't cease with his birth. She mothered him through his childhood and adolescence and accompanied him throughout his life, even to Calvary. As the Second Vatican Council said, "Thus in a very special way Mary cooperated by her obedience, faith, hope and burning charity in the work of the Savior in restoring supernatural life to souls. For this reason she is a mother to us in the order of grace" (*Lumen Gentium* 61). Our restoration to grace was entirely the work of Christ, but Mary's cooperation with him has left a Marian imprint on our salvation. The grace of salvation which comes entirely from Christ has a maternal aspect. Pope John Paul II writes:

And so, in the redemptive economy of grace, brought about through the action of the Holy Spirit, there is a unique correspondence between the moment of the Incarnation of the Word and the moment of the birth of the Church. The person who links these two moments is Mary: Mary at Nazareth and Mary in the Upper Room at Jerusalem. In both cases her discreet yet essential presence indicates the path of "birth from the Holy Spirit." Thus she who is present in the mystery of Christ as Mother becomes—by the will of her Son and the power of the Holy Spirit—present in the mystery of the Church. In the Church too she continues to be a maternal presence. (*Redemptoris mater* 24)

Mary is not just a memory in the church; she is a real, living, loving, caring maternal presence. This maternal presence takes an intercessory form. According to the Second Vatican Council, "This motherhood of Mary in the order of grace continues without interruption from the consent which she loyally gave at the Annunciation and which she sustained without wavering beneath the cross, until the eternal fulfillment of all the elect" (*Lumen Gentium* 62)

ℰᴓ

Mediation of Intercession

The church, then, clearly believes that just as Mary played an active role in the life and work of Jesus, so she plays an active role in the life and work of the church. She is present in the church as our sister but also as our spiritual mother. As the council said, "she cares for the brethren of her Son." Her maternal care is exercised through her intercession with her Son on our behalf. This does not imply that Jesus himself doesn't care or that he needs his mother to remind him to care, or that we cannot approach Jesus directly ourselves. It means that Jesus honors his mother and honors the role he gave to her when he declared that she is our mother. At Cana, Jesus honored the relationship Mary had with him as his mother when he responded to her request and provided wine for the wedding feast. Reflecting on this Gospel event, Pope John Paul II writes:

> The description of the Cana event outlines what is actually manifested as a new kind of motherhood according to the spirit and not just according to the flesh, that is to say Mary's solicitude for human beings, her coming to them in the wide variety of their wants and needs. At Cana in Galilee there is shown only one concrete aspect of human need, apparently a small one and of little importance ("They have no wine"). But it has a symbolic value: this coming to the aid of human needs means, at the same time, bringing those needs within the radius of Christ's messianic mission and salvific power. Thus there is a mediation: Mary places herself between her Son and mankind in the reality of their wants, needs and sufferings. *She puts herself "in the middle," that is to say she acts as a mediatrix not as an outsider, but in her position as mother.* She knows that she can point out to her Son the needs of mankind, and in fact she "has the right" to do so. Her mediation is thus in the nature of intercession: Mary "intercedes" for mankind. (*Redemptoris mater* 21)

Jesus accepts his mother's new role as our mother; he honors her concerns for us; he welcomes her as his mother when she brings into "the radius of his messianic mission and power" our needs; he welcomes her "mediation of intercession." That is the theological basis of Mary's mediation.

Mary's intercession with Jesus is not a substitute for Jesus' intercession with the Father. Her intercession is on the level of her motherhood, whereas Jesus' intercession is on the level of his divine sonship and his redemptive obedience. While Jesus stands before the Father, as our high priest, offering himself for our salvation, Mary stands before Jesus as his mother, interceding for us who have become her children through his word from the cross. Mary's spiritual motherhood is Christ's gift to us; her maternal intercession and mediation for us are Christ's gift to her. When he said to his mother, "Behold your son," he commissioned her to take care of all his disciples, and he endowed her with the grace of intercession for this task. The one mediator between God and us, Jesus Christ, gave his mother the grace of spiritual motherhood of all the faithful. Mary's mediation of intercession never takes the place of Christ's mediation of redemption. The council said:

> But Mary's function as mother of humankind in no way obscures or diminishes this unique mediation of Christ, but rather shows its power. All the Blessed Virgin's salutary influence on men and women originates not in any inner necessity but in the disposition of God. It flows forth from the superabundance of the merits of Christ, rests on his mediation, depends entirely on it and draws all its power from it. It does not hinder in any way the immediate union of the faithful with Christ but on the contrary fosters it. (*Lumen Gentium* 60)

This ecumenically sensitive statement is a clear expression of Catholic belief in Mary's "mediation of intercession." The Marian titles of Mediatrix of All Grace or Co-Redemptrix, which some hoped would be defined by the Second Vatican Council, were not developed by the council fathers. Pope Pius XII had received many requests for a dogmatic definition of Mary's mediation as "co-redemptrix" or "mediatrix of all graces." No one could accuse that great pope of being a minimalist in Marian teaching and devotion, yet he felt that this type of emphasis on Mary's mediation was not yet theologically clear enough or mature enough for such a definition. Vatican II agreed with him. This council took a very different approach to Mary. One of the great debates in the council concerned how to treat of Mary. Some bishops wanted the council to publish a separate document on Mary; others wanted the role of Mary to be discussed in the context of the church. When the matter was put to a vote in the council, the proposal that the role of Mary should be treated in the document on the church was carried by a very slim majority, 1114 to 1074.

Great saints and doctors of the church have preached about

Mary being the mediatrix of all graces. St. Bernard said, "God wills us to have everything through Mary." The influential books of *The True Devotion* by St. Louis Grignon de Montfort and *The Glories of Mary* by St. Alphonsus de Liguori are based on the conviction that we receive all grace through Mary's mediation. When the council failed to take up this belief in a more positive way and promote the understanding of Mary as our mediatrix, many Catholics were disappointed. The council, as quoted above, clearly stated the nature of Mary's mediation: "It flows forth from the superabundance of the merits of Christ, rests on his mediation, depends entirely on it and draws all its power from it." Mary's mediation is always subordinate to and dependent on the mediation of Christ. But Mary's mediation is real, it is efficacious, it is maternal. That is why the Vatican Council said,

> The Church does not hesitate to profess this subordinate role of Mary, which it constantly experiences and recommends to the heartfelt attention of the faithful, so that encouraged by this maternal help they may the more closely adhere to the Mediator and Redeemer. (*Lumen Gentium* 62)

Because Mary is our spiritual mother and mediates with her Son on our behalf, the church has always sought her powerful intercession. Mary's mediation is, in the words of Pope John Paul II, "a mediation of intercession." We do not say that no grace will be given if Mary doesn't ask; rather, we say that every grace for which Mary asks will be granted. Because she is our loving mother, always seeking our eternal salvation, Mary continues to intercede for us. She asks Jesus for all the graces we need. Hence, we can say that every grace we receive comes to us through the intercession of Mary our Mother. There is no grace that we need for which she doesn't ask. But that is a way of speaking about Mary's powerful intercession. It is not a doctrine that the church could at the present time define as a dogma of our faith. Her intercession with Jesus is, we believe, all-powerful. It would not become any more powerful if it were made a dogma of our faith. Mary's intercession with Jesus is all-powerful because she only asks according to the will of God. She knows that God wills each one of us to be saved. That is why she continually asks for all the graces we need to secure our eternal salvation. This awareness of Mary's powerful intercession is the basis of our devotion to Mary. In the rest of this book we will consider our devotion to Mary.

Devotion to Mary

EVOTION TO OUR BLESSED LADY is based on the word of God. It is our response to Jesus' last word to his beloved disciple and the fulfillment of Mary's own prophecy, "All generations will call me blessed." His last word to his disciple, his last will and testament, was expressed in the words "She is your mother." In a very striking comment on these words, Pope John Paul II said: "it can be said that by asking the beloved disciple to treat Mary as his mother Jesus founded Marian devotion."[1] Jesus asked his beloved disciple to be devoted to his mother, to have the same love, care, and respect for Mary as he himself had. That is the original meaning of the word "devotion." We often speak of someone being very devoted to father or mother. Some people conclude their letters with the phrase "I remain, Yours devotedly." Devotion involves thinking about, being attentive to, caring for, spending time with.

Being devoted to Mary doesn't mean being devoted to her memory, to the fact that she was the mother of Jesus, but being devoted to her person, to the one who is Mother of Jesus today and who is present in the mystery of Christ and the church today. Pope John Paul II writes:

> Mary is present in the Church as the Mother of Christ, and at the same time as that Mother whom Christ, in the mystery of the Redemption, gave to humanity in the person of the Apostle John. Thus, in her new motherhood in the Spirit, Mary embraces each and every one *in* the Church, and embraces each and every one *through* the Church. (*Redemptoris mater* 47)

Devotion to Mary involves a relationship with a living, loving person, present in our lives, whom we acknowledge to be our mother in the Spirit. Mary, now totally alive in God, is present to us in God as Mother of Christ and Mother of the Church, the Mystical Body of Christ. Her maternal presence fills us with confidence and hope. We know we can trust her. Pope John Paul II says, "For it must be recognized that before anyone else it was God himself, the Eternal Father, who *entrusted himself to the Virgin of Nazareth,* giving her his own Son in the mystery of the Incarnation" (*Redemptoris mater* 39). This remarkable teaching focuses on the reality behind all devotion to Mary: God the Father trusted her and entrusted his Son to her. Our devotion is a sign that we too trust her and that we entrust ourselves to her.

The notion of "entrusting" is a major theme of the pope's teaching. The Father entrusts his Son to Mary; Jesus entrusts his disciple (all disciples) to Mary; we entrust ourselves to Mary. What is "entrusting"? John Paul defines it in this way: "Such entrusting is *the response* to a person's love, and in particular *to a mother's love*" (*Redemptoris mater* 45). It is to the love of Mary that the Father entrusts Jesus in the mystery of the incarnation; it is to the love of Mary that Jesus entrusts the disciple in the mystery of the church. God himself recognizes Mary's love as a safe place, a healthy and nourishing environment for his Son. Jesus, having experienced that love throughout his life, confidently entrusts his disciple to Mary's care. Pope John Paul II writes:

> The Redeemer entrusts Mary to John because he entrusts John to Mary. At the foot of the Cross there begins that special entrusting of humanity to the mother of Christ, which in the history of the Church has been practiced and expressed in different ways. (*Redemptoris mater* 45)

When we look at God the Father's trusting attitude toward Mary, and when we reflect on how Jesus, having experienced the love of his mother, entrusts us to her love, we cannot avoid the question: Do we entrust ourselves to Mother Mary's love? Do we recognize and celebrate our relationship with Mary our Mother? John Paul says,

> The Marian dimension of the life of a disciple of Christ is
> expressed in a special way precisely through this filial entrust-
> ing to the Mother of Christ, which began with the testament
> of the Redeemer on Golgotha. Entrusting himself to Mary in
> a filial manner, the Christian, like the Apostle John, "wel-
> comes" the Mother of Christ "into his own home" and brings
> her into everything that makes up his inner life, that is to say
> into his human and Christian "I": *he took her into his own
> home.* (*Redemptoris mater* 45)

That means that when I become conscious of myself as a Christian,
redeemed by Christ on the cross, I become conscious too that in
that very hour of redemption, Jesus gave me Mary as my mother.

The act of entrusting oneself to Mary with love and confidence is the clearest way of recognizing and honoring our deepest relationship with her: she is our mother in the order of the
new creation, the order of grace. Our devotion to Our Lady
begins with this recognition. True devotion will always be rooted
in this spiritual relationship, which inspires in us the confidence
to entrust ourselves to Mary. The act of entrusting has its origin
in Christ and always leads to Christ. John Paul writes: "This filial
relationship, this self-entrusting of a child to its mother not only
has its *beginning in Christ* but can also be said to be *definitely
directed towards him.* Mary can be said to continue to say to each
individual the words she spoke at Cana in Galilee: Do whatever
he tells you" (*Redemptoris mater* 45). All true forms of devotion
to Mary are expressions of this entrustment, this "taking Mary
into one's own home."

℘

The Communion of Saints

St. Thomas Aquinas wrote, "Devotion is apparently nothing else
but the will to give oneself readily to things concerning the service of God" (*Summa Theologiae* II–II, q. 82, art. 1). God is always
at the center of devotion. True devotion to Mary is always a man-

ifestation of one's eagerness to serve God. Entrusting oneself to Mary, who is in God, is an expression of a desire to entrust oneself more radically to God. As St. Thomas said, "Devotion to God's holy ones, dead or living, does not terminate in them, but passes to God, in so far as we honor God in His servants" (ibid., art. 2 ad 2). Behind our devotion to Mary is our faith in "the communion of saints."

Jesus didn't come to us in an individualistic way. He came as a son of Abraham, son of David, son of Mary, as a member of God's people. In a purely individualistic notion of salvation, where I would be aware of only God and myself, devotion would be exclusively to God or to Christ. But although Christ alone is my Savior, Christ is never alone. He is the head of his body, the church. We are all members of his body and therefore members of one another. God didn't choose to save us in an individualistic way. As the Second Vatican Council said:

> God willed to make women and men holy and save them, not as individuals without any bond or link between them, but rather to make them into a people who might acknowledge him and serve him in holiness. (*Lumen Gentium* 9)

As members of the People of God, we all share common ancestry and acknowledge Abraham, in the words of St. Paul, "the ancestor of all believers" (Rom. 4:12); as members of the Body of Christ we are interrelated, brothers and sisters in Christ, and give respect and reverence to each other, and especially to those great champions of the faith, the saints, who have gone before us. In praising them we are acknowledging the victory of God's grace in them; in asking for their intercession we are putting into practice the faith that we profess when we say, "We believe in the communion of saints." Catholic devotion to Mary and the saints is deeply rooted in the Catholic vision of the church as the communion of saints. In asking Mary or the saints to pray for us, we are reminding ourselves that what God has done in them he can also do in us. Far from corrupting our worship of God, true devotion to Our Lady is a constant reminder of the sovereignty of God's grace in Christ, the absolute gratuitousness of salvation, and the one unique sacrifice that the Son of Mary offered to God for our forgiveness and justification. Pope Paul VI wrote:

> The Catholic Church, endowed with centuries of experience, recognizes in devotion to the Blessed Virgin a powerful aid for women and men as they strive for fulfillment. Mary, the New Woman, stands at the side of Christ, the New Man, within whose mystery the mystery of human beings alone finds true light; she is given to us as a pledge and guarantee that God's Plan in Christ for the salvation of the whole person has already achieved realization in a creature: in her. Contemplated in the episodes of the Gospels and in the reality which she already possesses in the City of God, the Blessed Virgin Mary offers a calm vision and a reassuring word to modern people, torn as they often are between anguish and hope, defeated by the sense of their own limitations and assailed by limitless aspirations, troubled in their minds and divided in their heart, uncertain before the riddle of death, oppressed by loneliness while yearning for fellowship, a prey to boredom and disgust. She shows forth the victory of hope over anguish, of fellowship over solitude, of peace over anxiety, of joy and beauty over boredom and disgust, of eternal visions over earthly ones, of life over death. (*To Honor Mary* 59)

Devotion to Mary—contemplating the victory of God's redeeming love in Mary, belonging to all the generations who call Mary blessed—has existed in the church from the earliest times. Jesus' will that his disciples should be devoted to his mother began to form in the consciousness of the early church those attitudes of love, trust, and confidence that are the essential features of Marian devotion. We cannot say with certainty when devotion to Mary began. Some modern scholars claim that, even when St. Luke was writing the Gospel that bears his name, there was a public veneration of Mary in his community. His community must have been calling Mary blessed because St. Luke placed on Mary's lips the prophecy "All generations will call me blessed." St. Luke would hardly have attributed this prophecy to Mary if his own generation, his own community of Christians, seventy or eighty years after she first sang her Magnificat, was not already calling Mary blessed. John McHugh suggests that Elizabeth's greeting to Mary, "Of all women you are the most blessed and blessed is the fruit of your womb" (Luke 1:42), was the opening line of a hymn in honor of Mary.[2] In Luke's Gospel, too, an unnamed woman in the crowd praised Mary: "Blessed is the womb that bore you" (Luke 11:27–28). While Jesus directed her to the true source of blessing, "the hearing of the word of God," it is also true to say, in the words of Pope John Paul II, that "this unnamed woman was the first to confirm unwittingly that prophetic phrase of Mary's *Magnificat* and to begin the *Magnificat* of the ages" (*Redemptoris mater* 20).

Without getting involved in the debate over when devotion to Our Lady began, or when the first historical evidence of this devotion emerged, the Second Vatican Council stated:

> From the earliest times the Blessed Virgin is honoured under the title of Mother of God, under whose protection the faithful take refuge together in prayer in all their perils and needs. Accordingly, following the Council of Ephesus, there was a remarkable growth in the cult of the People of God towards Mary, in veneration and love, in invocation and imitation, according to the prophetic words: "all generations shall call me blessed." This cult, as it has always existed in the Church, for all its uniqueness, differs essentially from the cult of adoration, which is offered equally to the Incarnate Word and to the Father and the Holy Spirit, and is most favorable to it. The various forms of piety towards the Mother of God, which the Church has approved within the limits of sound and orthodox doctrine, according to the dispositions and understanding of the faithful, ensure that while the mother is honored, the Son through whom all things have their being (cf. Col. 1:16) and in whom it has pleased the Father that all fullness should dwell (cf. Col. 1:19) is rightly known, loved and glorified and his commandments are observed. (*Lumen Gentium* 66)

The council, in a note on "from the earliest times" refers to the *Sub tuum praesidium,* the prayer that we know as, "We fly to thy protection, O holy Mother of God, despise not our petitions in our necessities, but deliver us from all danger, O ever glorious and blessed Virgin." The Greek version of this prayer dates from the beginning of the third century. If this prayer had already been written down—and writing was not all that common in those days—the Christians of Alexandria in Egypt could have been saying that prayer from as early as the second century. Surely it is very significant that at this very early stage in the development of the church, only decades after the death of John the Evangelist, Christians were turning with confidence to Our Lady and asking for her powerful intercession. That confidence in Mary's intercession is the secret of all devotion to Mary. In the Catholic Church we have always believed that that confidence is inspired in us by the Holy Spirit. Devotion to Mary is a gift of the Spirit. As the Second Vatican Council said, "The Catholic Church taught by the Holy Spirit, honors her with filial affection and devotion as a most beloved mother" (*Lumen Gentium* 52). Since devotion is a gift of the Holy Spirit we should, in principle, be open to receive and welcome it.

༄

The Orthodox Churches

Devotion to Mary has taken many forms throughout the history of the church. To this day the Orthodox Church of the East is famous for its great devotion to the Mother of God, the *Theotokos;* its liturgical praise of Mary is noted for its exuberance; its icons of the Virgin and Child are renowned for their beauty and religious sensitivity; its hymns in honor of Mary, such as the *Akathistos,* are incomparable and express the living tradition of the people's love and veneration of Mary. The Orthodox bishop Kallistos Ware said:

> That we should turn to Mary in prayer seems to an Orthodox Christian something altogether natural and inevitable. For him there is nothing exotic or polemical about such prayer, but it forms an integral and unquestioned part of his life in

Christ. He does not think of such prayers in legalist categories, attempting to measure divine grace or employing the concept of "merit"; nor does he think of it in a sentimental fashion, as if Mary were more "lenient" and "indulgent" than her Son. For Orthodoxy, this prayer springs quite simply from the sense of "belonging together," from the feeling that we and she are members of the same fellowship, that she is Mother within the great Christian family of which we are also part. We and she belong to the one Church, and the unity of that Church is a unity of prayer—that, in a word, is why we ask her to pray for us.[3]

The Orthodox make a distinction between "invoking Mary" and "praying to Mary." We do not pray, they say, in the strict sense, "to Mary"; we pray only "to God." But we ask Mary for her prayers or we invoke her intercession. As Ware says,

Our belief as Orthodox concerning the Mother of God is expressed above all through the medium of prayer and worship. *Lex orandi lex credendi;* our faith is disclosed through, and conditioned by, the way in which we pray. In the words of Archpriest George Florovsky, "Christianity is first of all a worshipping community. Worship comes first, doctrine and disciple second." If this is true of Orthodox theology in general, it is true in a special sense of the Orthodox approach to the Theotokos. The mystery of the Mother of God is par excellence a liturgical mystery.[4]

Whoever enters an Orthodox church sees immediately the place of honor given to Our Lady. On the screen separating the sanctuary from the body of the church, known as the iconostasis, there is a large icon depicting Christ as a child in the arms of his Mother. It is an icon of the incarnation. Another icon depicts Christ enthroned with Mary and John the Baptist standing on either side with their heads bowed and their hands raised in intercession. Here we see the Mother of Christ as a member of the church, with Christ's great precursor, interceding on our behalf. Ware makes the comment: "Better than any verbal explanation, these two icons will help him to understand the place of the

Mother of God in the scheme of redemption."[5] She is Mother of Christ; she intercedes with Christ on our behalf. That is why Christians of the Orthodox churches have always turned to her with confidence and love.

℘

The Protestant Reformation

The Protestant Reformation disrupted the unity of the Latin church, the Western church, in the sixteenth century. Catholics recognize today that the church badly needed reform. There were many abuses. Regrettably, the much-needed reform took the form of division. The Protestant Reform movement became independent Protestant churches, separated from the Catholic Church. One of the casualties of the Reformation battles and subsequent religious conflict was devotion to Our Lady among many if not most Protestants. Martin Luther himself maintained his own personal devotion to Mary. He wrote a beautiful commentary on the Magnificat and preached some sixty sermons on Our Lady.

As the Reformed churches developed, especially in the climate of religious wars and conflicts that accompanied the Reformation in the sixteenth and seventeenth centuries, religious practices that became the hallmark of one tradition were rejected by the other. For instance, the Bible became the hallmark of Protestantism. "The Bible alone" became a religious slogan. Catholics, in response, shunned the Bible and turned instead to the Catechism and the teaching of the church. Devotion to Mary became the hallmark of Catholics. In response, Protestants tended to shun all devotion to the Mother of God and to level accusations of "mariolatry," worship of Mary, against Catholics. Even when the religious wars ceased, the theological wars over doctrine continued right up until the time of the Second Vatican Council. A very strong Marian movement developed in the Cath-

olic Church, culminating in the definition of two new dogmas
of faith, the Immaculate Conception of Our Blessed Lady and the
Assumption of Our Lady into heaven. Protestants of all denomi-
nations objected very strongly to the promulgation of these dogmas. The more overtly Marian the Catholic Church became, the
less Marian the Protestant churches had to appear.

The Second Vatican Council signaled an end to religious
conflict among Christians. Not only was it a watershed in the life
of the Catholic Church; it was also ecumenically the dawn of
new relationships between the Catholic Church and the
Protestant churches and churches of the Anglican Communion.
In just over thirty years the new ecumenical spirit has dispelled
the spirit of fear and bigotry; genuine dialogue has begun; col-
laboration on all levels is bearing fruit; Christians of all denom-
inations now belong to ecumenical groups, faith-sharing groups,
prayer groups, and, most encouragingly from the perspective of
this chapter, to the Ecumenical Society of the Blessed Virgin
Mary. As Catholics and Protestants return to the common source
of their faith, to the Word of God, and to the earliest creeds, general councils, and fathers of the church, they are beginning to
share again a common vision of Mary. The Lutheran–Roman
Catholic Dialogue in the United States has already produced two
major studies: *Mary in the New Testament* and *The One Mediator,
the Saints and Mary.* In Britain we have the publications of the
papers delivered at the meetings of the Ecumenical Society of the
Blessed Virgin Mary.

---

§∂

Lutherans

Mother Basilea Schlink, who founded the Evangelical Sisterhood
of Mary within the German Lutheran Church after the Second
World War, records the change of attitude which she has experienced with regard to Mary:

When Martin Luther bids us to praise the mother Mary, declaring that she can never be praised enough as the noblest lady and, after Christ, the fairest gem in Christendom, I must confess that for many years I was one of those who had not done so, although Scripture says that henceforth all generations would call Mary blessed (Luke 1:48). I had not taken my place among these generations. . . . By the grace of the Lord I have in the past few decades increasingly learnt to love and revere the mother Mary the more I contemplated her life on the basis of Holy Scripture. It is my prayer that the Lord may use this book so that among us Protestants Mary, the mother of the Lord, will once again receive the love and honour that are her due according to Holy Scripture and as the reformer Martin Luther has impressed upon our hearts.[6]

This prayer, and the prayers of many others like Mother Basilea, are being answered. The official dialogue between Lutherans and Roman Catholics in the United States has advanced understanding of Marian devotion in a remarkable way. The Catholic theologians involved in this dialogue state:

One obstacle to full communion is the suspicion sometimes voiced by Lutherans and others that the invocation of saints and the honor paid to Mary in the Catholic Church are idolatrous and injurious to the honor that belongs to God alone. We believe that in the light of the teaching of Vatican II, reinforced by many statements of Paul VI and John Paul II, it may be possible for Lutherans to declare that such accusations are today unwarranted. We are gratified that the Lutherans of this dialogue join us in recommending that their church authorities make an acknowledgement to that effect.[7]

In response to this request the Lutheran theologians wrote:

We have learnt that Roman Catholics made a serious distinction between worship (latria, for God) and veneration (dulia, for saints; hyperdulia, for Mary) and that they have a long tradition of fighting against abuses in worship and piety. We have also learned in this dialogue how incorrect it is for

Lutherans to disdain Roman Catholic piety regarding the saints and Mary and simply condemn it as idolatry.[8]

Catholics will be greatly encouraged by this report from the Lutheran–Roman Catholic Dialogue in the United States. They will know that their Lutheran brothers and sisters accept their devotion to Mary as a legitimate expression of the veneration that they themselves have in their hearts for the Mother of the Lord, even though they don't express their veneration in "Catholic ways." Ecumenically sensitive Catholics will also be relieved to know that their devotion to Our Lady is not a barrier to deep dialogue with the Lutheran Church.

ॐ

The Anglican Communion

In the worldwide Anglican Communion there has always been a great diversity of attitudes to Mary, ranging from very Catholic devotions such as the Rosary and pilgrimages to a relative silence about her in both private and public devotion. Edward Yarnold, S.J., gives us a very useful summary of the areas of agreement between the Anglican Communion and the Catholic Church:

1. Mary's role must not be interpreted so as to obscure the fact that Jesus Christ is the one Mediator between God and us (1 Tim. 2:5).

2. Christian understanding of Mary is inseparably linked with the doctrines of Christ and the church.

3. Mary, as Mother of God incarnate, received a unique vocation.

4. God prepared her by his grace to be the mother of the Savior, by whom she was herself redeemed. (This thesis expresses much of what Roman Catholics affirm in the dogma of the Immaculate Conception.)

5. She has already entered into the glory of heaven. (This thesis expresses much of what Roman Catholics affirm in the dogma of the Assumption.)

6. Both churches honor Mary in the communion of saints and observe liturgical feasts in her honor.

7. Mary is a "model of holiness, obedience and faith for Christians." She can therefore be regarded as a "prophetic figure of the Church."[9]

Catholics and Anglicans are already united in many areas of belief with regard to the Mother of God. There are, of course, areas of theological disagreement such as the dogmatic definitions of the Immaculate Conception and the Assumption, which must not be minimized. Patient dialogue between the two churches is making progress. However, in the actual pastoral and devotional life we can find almost total agreement. For example, when I asked a friend of mine, the vicar of an Anglican parish in England to describe his "devotion and the devotion of his parishioners to Our Lady" he wrote as follows:

> How can an Anglican Christian have devotion to Mary? How can we pray to her, asking her intercession for us? I mean, didn't Archbishop Cranmer's right-hand man Thomas Cromwell make sure there was a good old stripping of the altars and a mighty destruction of all statues and images? Surely what he began, Oliver Cromwell and his partners finished off during the Commonwealth times? Yes, that is no doubt true.
>
> But the gospel won't go away, nor will the vital role that God gave to Mary within that gospel record. That for me has been the base-line. It is the powerful, the mighty, the rich he (the Lord) sends away empty and Mary for whom he does great things. So how, you ask me, do I come to this faith? Not straight away. Much more by a process of reflection and experience.
>
> Clearly as a young priest, I would dutifully preach on Mary as an example of all kinds of virtues. But that is a long way from "Our Lady" who is alive in the Lord, and with whom I

pray the rosary, and with whose friends I meet to pray in that way. I think the making of several pilgrimages to the Shrine of Our Lady at Walsingham is probably very important to me. The devotion, Marian devotion, there is plain, open, palpable. I find it very beautiful, strangely moving, and resonating in the depths within me. But it's the people, often poorer people who pray the rosary who bring a new conversion of heart. The gentle, quiet almost ripple of prayer in a rosary group is strangely beautiful.

Love for the mother of the Lord Jesus, I found, cannot be instructed; it can only be absorbed. And in my case I found Marian devotion is not something I have long arguments about in my immediate Anglican circle. It is just there, like Mary is just there—for us as she was for Jesus. His mother and mine too, by adoption and grace.

A recent convert was quoted in a national daily paper. What he said rings bells for me: "I was also drawn by the Church's reverence for Mary and by the humanity of the saints. It seemed a very human church. It stirred my faith, my head and my heart." I say Amen to that.

This beautiful testimony describes how one pastoral priest found devotion to Mary for himself and how he is sharing it with his parishioners. I could discern no difference at all between his attitude to Mary and my own. He would, of course, be the first to point out that not every priest in the Anglican Communion would be leading his or her people along this Marian road. (Not every Catholic priest would be leading his parish along that road either.) But the fact is that there are many such priests in the Anglican Communion, and we can rejoice with them because they are restoring devotion to Mary to their church. Dogmatic problems with regard to Mary, especially the use of papal authority in promulgating the dogmas of the Immaculate Conception and the Assumption, remain unresolved difficulties in the Roman Catholic–Anglican Dialogue. But as Catholics and members of the Anglican Communion meet to share their devotion to Our Lady, the theological problems become secondary and solutions will be found.

ℬ

Presbyterians

The Presbyterian Church has its own very distinctive liturgical and devotional life. I asked a friend, a well-known minister in the Church of Scotland to outline how his congregation would relate to Mary. He kindly replied as follows:

> Most Presbyterians who worship regularly within the fellowship of the Church have a distant and remote relationship to Mary. Mary is not the focus of their faith and their devotion and many weeks could pass in a Presbyterian Church without any reference being made to Mary or indeed any mention of her name. When reference is made to Mary it might be in the context of:
>
> 1. *Saying the Apostles Creed* or the repetition of a recently authorised "Statement of Faith": "We proclaim Jesus Christ, God the Son, born of Mary by the power of the Holy Spirit" (General Assembly 1992). Such a confession of faith might only be used on special occasions, e.g. Baptism, Communion, Confirmation, Ordination.
>
> 2. *In the context of singing.* Hymns from the Church Hymnary (3rd edition) sections on Christ's Incarnation, Christ's life and ministry, Christ's passion and cross. Several hymns make specific reference to Mary.
>
> 3. *In the context of Advent,* when most ministers, I think, would preach about Mary. Expository preaching through the whole books of the Bible is still a custom in many churches. If a minister were expounding Mark's Gospel then he or she would make reference to Mary in the context of a particular passage.
>
> In 1994 the Panel on Worship produced "Common Order" in which there are prayers for five morning services—prayers of adoration, confession, thanksgiving and intercession. In the five orders of service there are only two references to Mary:

1. Prayer of Invocation
   "Son of the loveliest Mary light a flame of love in our hearts."
2. Prayers of Intercession
   "For the world we pray. May the Son of Mary move through all the earth, blessing it."

In response to the question "What is your attitude to the Virgin Mary" I was given the following responses—all from people who worship regularly:

"Well, she was the mother of Jesus, wasn't she?"

"It must have been pretty difficult for her being pregnant and not married, especially in a small village."

"Since she was Jesus' mother it means Jesus was really human."

"She must have gone through hell when Jesus was crucified."

"She was the first disciple."

"If she hadn't agreed to go along with God's plan there would be no Christianity."

"Obviously she was a woman of great faith and endurance."

Presbyterians, then, have their own distinctive way of remembering Mary in the mystery of Christ. We can see in the responses of the people their reverence for and understanding of Mary. As the bishops of the United States wrote, "We are convinced that all Christians share a basic reverence for the Mother of Jesus, a veneration deeper than doctrinal differences and theological disputes" (*She Is Your Mother* 106).

ℰ

Methodists

J. Neville Ward, the Methodist writer of the much-acclaimed book on the Rosary *Five for Sorrow Ten for Joy,* gives as his second reason for writing on the Rosary the following:

The second and clearly related reason is that in Methodism the silence about the Mother of Jesus is positively deafening. It is so complete that during a ministry of over thirty years I have begun to wonder what anxiety is behind this surprising mental hang-up. This wonder has increased as I have learned how much she means in the public and private praying of both the Roman Catholic and Orthodox Churches and, incidentally but importantly, as I begin to discover among our own people signs of shy but nervous interest in her mysterious being.[10]

Twenty-five years after Neville Ward wrote those words, that "shy but nervous interest in her mysterious being" has blossomed into a beautiful document prepared by the British Methodist–Roman Catholic committee. The document is entitled *Mary, Mother of the Lord: Sign of Grace, faith and holiness. Towards a shared understanding.* The opening paragraph of this document sets the ecumenical tone:

Christians increasingly seek to walk together on the pilgrim journey to holiness, moving from mutual suspicion to a genuine sharing of our different riches and insights. As we do so Mary, humble handmaid of the Lord and yet by God's own election and grace the human mother of our one Lord and Saviour, Jesus Christ, is more widely accepted as a powerful sign or "icon" of all that we are and can become as the people of God, the Church of Christ. There are both Methodists and Catholics who participate together, for example, in the Ecumenical Society of the Blessed Virgin Mary. We acknowledge, however, that whereas Catholics affirm the Marian doctrines as part of the development of doctrine, these doctrines are not found in the Methodist tradition, and Methodists in general have not discussed such questions in any great depth. Facing the issues involved is part of the ecumenical challenge. (§3)

From this common ground of seeing Mary as "a powerful sign or icon of all that we can become" Catholics can now share their faith with Methodists in the knowledge that their devotion to Mary will not be an obstacle to fruitful dialogue. As this joint Catholic–Methodist statement says:

Motherhood is a permanent relationship. Now that Christians
are incorporated into Christ, united to our Head as his Body,
Mary can be seen as the Mother of all Christians and of the
Church. From the cross, Christ can be seen as giving Mary a
maternal relation to all believers as symbolised by John:
"Woman, behold your son: son, behold your mother" (John
19:26). Mary is the mother of the "whole Christ." Head and
members together, but she remains at the same time a fellow
disciple and our sister in God's family. (§6)

As Methodists and Catholics share about this "maternal relation" that Mary has with all Christians, a deeper understanding
will emerge. Methodists will come to understand Catholic devotion, and Catholics will begin to understand Methodist reservations and even opposition to certain forms or expressions of that
devotion.

ℱ𝕒

Marian Devotions and Ecumenism

We Catholics have to remind ourselves that the church has
always opposed all forms of what the Second Vatican Council
called "vain credulity"; it has also resisted all forms of exaggeration with regard to Mary's influence, for example, the totally
false notion that Mary is more approachable than Jesus or that
Mary can command Jesus to do her will. Catholics may not be
too disturbed by these pious and foolish exaggerations, as we
know the hyperbolic nature of them, but many Protestants are
offended and are unable to understand. The Vatican Council
strongly urged

> theologians and preachers of the word of God to be careful to
> refrain as much from all false exaggeration as from too sum-
> mary an attitude in considering the special dignity of the
> Mother of God. Following the study of sacred scripture, the
> Fathers, the doctors and the liturgy of the Church, and under
> the guidance of the Church's magisterium, let them rightly

illustrate the offices and privileges of the Blessed Virgin which always refer to Christ, the source of all truth, sanctity, and devotion. Let them carefully refrain from whatever might by word or deed lead the separated sisters and brothers or any others whatsoever into error about the true doctrine of the Church. (*Lumen Gentium* 9)

For this reason Pope Paul VI laid great emphasis on the right ordering of devotion to Mary. He said specifically that we must avoid all such exaggerations. And he gave us four criteria for the development of a healthy and sound devotion.

1. *Biblical.* Paul VI said, "Today it is recognized as a general need of Christian piety that every form of worship should have a biblical imprint. Devotion to the Blessed Virgin cannot be exempted from this general orientation of Christian piety; indeed it should draw inspiration in a special way from this general orientation in order to gain new vigour and sure help."

2. *Liturgical.* "Devotions should be so drawn up that they harmonize with the liturgical seasons, accord with the sacred liturgy, are in some way derived from it, and lead the people to it, since in fact the liturgy by its very nature is far superior to any of them."

3. *Ecumenical.* "The ecumenical aspect of Marian devotion is shown in the Catholic Church's desire that, without in any way detracting from the unique character of this devotion, every care should be taken to avoid any exaggeration which could mislead other Christian brethren about the true nature of the Catholic Church. Similarly, the Church desires that any manifestation of cult which is opposed to correct Catholic practice should be eliminated."

4. *Anthropological.* "When the Church considers the long history of Marian devotion she rejoices at the continuity of the element of cult which it shows, but she does not bind herself to any particular expression of an individual

cultural epoch or to the particular anthropological ideas underlying such expressions. The Church understands that certain outward religious expressions, while perfectly valid in themselves, may be less suitable to the men and women of different ages and cultures." (*To Honor Mary* 2)

Incorporating these criteria into the expression of our Marian devotion will be an ecumenical development of great significance and will produce forms of devotion that will be attractive to all Christians. All we need for true devotion is what the word of God says about Mary in Scripture. As St. Thérèse of Lisieux said, "If a sermon on the Holy Virgin is to bear fruit, it must show her real life as the Gospel makes us see it, and not her supposed life; and we can guess that her real life, at Nazareth and later, must have been quite ordinary."[11] While we honor Mary as Queen of Heaven and Earth, Mary herself would never want us to overlook the fact that she is the "lowly handmaid of the Lord." And if we wish to give her true honor, then we listen to her voice as she says, "Do whatever he tells you." True devotion to Mary consists in doing what Jesus asks of us.

6

Mary in the Public Worship of the Church

HROUGHOUT THE LITURGICAL YEAR, the Catholic Church celebrates worldwide fifteen feasts of Our Blessed Lady. There are
many national and local feasts of Mary as well. For instance the
feast of Our Lady of Perpetual Help, not mentioned in the universal calendar, is widely celebrated in those countries where
there is a devotion to Our Lady under this title.

Liturgical feasts began as celebrations by the people of some
truth or event in the life of Christ, Our Lady, or the saints. As A.
Agnus observes:

> Marian liturgical recognition was not occasioned by a series
> of feasts imposed from above: it was the acceptance of popu-
> lar acclamation exerting pressure from below. . . . It was the
> faithful drawing upon the Holy Scriptures, who first appre-
> hended the Marian prerogatives: these were elaborated by the
> Fathers and Scripture Commentators (such as Origen †254 AD)
> and then, thereby, the beliefs found their place in the liturgy.[1]

Pope Paul VI devoted a whole encyclical to Mary's place in the
liturgy of the church. In this encyclical he reminds us that "both
in the East and in the West the highest and purest expressions of
devotion to the Blessed Virgin have sprung from the liturgy or

[I depend greatly in this chapter on the excellent book by Fr. Christopher
O'Donnell, *With Mary at Worship* (Wilmington, Del.: Michael Glazier, 1988). I am
especially indebted to him for the way in which he marshaled church documents
in his treatment of the various feasts. The book by J. D. Creighton, *Our Lady in
the Liturgy* (Dublin, 1997) offers many helpful insights.]

111

have been incorporated into it" (*To Honor Mary* 15). In the same encyclical, he also points out that the liturgy protects devotion to Mary from "vain credulity." He tells us that "the Church desires to live the mystery of Christ with Mary."

In the Constitution on the Sacred Liturgy, the Second Vatican Council, reflecting on Mary's place in the liturgical year, said:

> In celebrating the annual cycle of the mysteries of Christ, the church honors the blessed Mary, Mother of God, with a special love. She is inseparably linked with her Son's saving work. In her the church admires and exalts the most excellent fruit of redemption, and joyfully contemplates, as in a faultless image, the goal it anticipates and desires for all its members. (*Sacrosanctum Concilium* 103)

In this chapter we will look at the fifteen feasts of Our Lady that the church celebrates universally. Our purpose here is to reflect on both the doctrinal and the devotional context of these feasts. But we will not consider each feast on an equal basis, because in the liturgical calendar four feasts are called Solemnities, three are called Feasts, and eight are called Optional Memorials. While indicating when the Optional Memorials occur, I will reflect, for reasons of space, only on the Solemnities and the Feasts. The question to keep in mind as we review this rich liturgical source of doctrine and devotion is this: How does the liturgy of these feasts form and foster in the church not just a Marian devotion but a Marian attitude of mind and heart? Mary, of course, is remembered every day during the celebration of Holy Mass. In the first Eucharistic Prayer of the ancient Roman Canon, we say, "In union with the whole Church we honor Mary, the ever Virgin Mother of Jesus Christ our Lord and God." In the third Eucharistic Prayer we say, "May he make us an everlasting gift to you [the Father] and enable us to share in the inheritance of your saints, with Mary, the ever Virgin Mother of God." Her presence throughout the church's year is also very evident, especially during the season of Advent.

ৡৡ

Mary, Mother of God
Solemnity, 1 January

New Year's Day, a public holiday in many countries, provides the church with the opportunity of celebrating the first big feast in honor of Our Lady. New Year's Day, while being the start of the civil year, is also the octave of Christmas Day, the birth of Christ. On this day the faithful of the Catholic Church assemble for Mass to deepen their faith in the reality of the mystery of the incarnation by celebrating a feast in honor of Mary the Mother of Jesus, the Mother of God. In the entrance antiphon the congregation greets Our Lady with the words, "Hail, Holy Mother! The child to whom you gave birth is the king of heaven and earth." The church teaches us always to combine our acclaim of Mary our "Holy Mother" with a confession of faith in the divinity of her Son. With this proclamation of faith in Jesus and reverence for his Mother we are open to hear and be blessed by the word of God.

The first reading is from Numbers 6:22–27. God reveals to Moses how Aaron should bless the people: "May Yahweh bless you and keep you. May Yahweh let his face shine on you and be gracious to you. May Yahweh show you his face and bring you peace." It is surely appropriate that on the day when we celebrate the divine motherhood of Mary, whose Son brings God's blessing of salvation to the whole world, the liturgy should place before us this triune blessing. On New Year's Day we wish each other a happy New Year. This feast of the divine motherhood is the source of all our happiness because the love, joy, and peace that our souls crave come to us through Mary's Child.

The Son of God was born of the Blessed Virgin Mary so that we could be born of God. Our rebirth comes through the Holy Spirit, who has been poured into our hearts. In the second reading of this feast, from Galatians 4:4–7, the word of God says "when the completion of time came, God sent his Son, born of a woman, born subject to the Law, to redeem the subjects of the Law and to enable us to be adopted as sons. The proof that you are sons is that God has sent the Spirit of his Son into our hearts: the Spirit that cries 'Abba, Father.'" Commenting on these words Pope John Paul writes: "They are words which celebrate together the love of the Father, the mission of the Son, the gift of the Holy Spirit, the role of the woman from whom the Redeemer was born, and our own divine filiation in the mystery of the fullness of time" (*Redemptoris mater* 1). We begin each new year remembering and celebrating how Our Lady has cooperated with the Father, the Son, and the Holy Spirit in the great work of our redemption. Through her willingness and cooperation, through her divine motherhood "God sent his Son."

The Gospel of the Mass for the day, Luke 2:16–21, shows us Mary in her most characteristic mode, that is, pondering in her heart. The shepherds were chosen by God to proclaim the birth of Christ. The Gospel says, "Everyone who heard it was astonished at what the shepherds said to them." From among all those who heard, Mary is singled out: "As for Mary, she treasured all these things and pondered them in her heart." It is only by pondering God's word that we grow in faith. What happened to all those who "were astonished at what the shepherds said"? Being "astonished" is not enough. Jesus said, "Blessed are those who hear the word and keep it."

The feast of the divine motherhood celebrates the central truth of Christian faith: God became human and was born of Mary. The surest way to grow in this faith is to celebrate it. We saw how the church, in the early centuries, struggled to defend, clarify, and hand on faith in the divine motherhood of Mary. As we related above, eventually the Council of Ephesus in 431 decreed: "If anyone does not confess that Emmanuel is truly God and therefore that the blessed Virgin is truly Mother of God (*Theotokos*) for she bore according to the flesh him who is the Word of God, let him be anathema." In the calm after the often hectic celebrations of Christmas, the church invites us to take a fresh look in faith at the mystery of the incarnation by celebrating the feast of Mary the Mother of God. St. Athanasius comments: "The Word 'took to himself descent from Abraham,' as the Apostle says, 'and therefore it was essential that he should in this way become completely like his brothers,' and take a body similar to us. That is why Mary is really part of his plan, so that he may take this body from her and offer it up for us as something of his own" (Office of Readings, 1 January).

The Second Vatican Council said, "Mary advanced in her pilgrimage of faith and faithfully persevered in her union with her Son until she stood at the cross" (*Lumen Gentium* 58). In this feast, as we begin the New Year, we join Mary on her pilgrimage. Her child has been born; she treasures what is said about him in her heart; she wants to teach us to do the same.

℘

The Presentation of the Lord
Feast, 2 February

This feast has been traditionally known as Candlemas Day. Candles are blessed and carried in procession. Candles not only create light but also are a symbol of light, a symbol of Christ "the light of the world." St. Sophronius, in his commentary in the Office of today says, "The most chaste Virgin Mother of God bore in her arms the true light and came to the help of those who were lying in darkness. In the same way we must hurry out to meet him who is truly light, enlightened by the beams of his brightness and bearing in our hands the light which shines for all men" (Office of Readings, 2 February).

In this feast we see Mary continuing her "pilgrimage of faith." She carries her child to Jerusalem to present him to the Lord in the temple. The significance of Mary's entrance into the temple with Jesus is highlighted in the first reading from Malachi 3:1–4: "I shall send my messenger to clear a way before me. And suddenly the Lord whom you seek will come to his Temple." Jesus, the Lord, now enters the temple in the arms of his mother. Those who are led by the Spirit of God will recognize him. They are represented by Simeon. The Gospel, from Luke 2:22–40, says, "It had been revealed to him [Simeon] by the Holy Spirit that he would not see death until he had set eyes on the Christ of the Lord. Prompted by the Holy Spirit he came to the Temple; and when the parents of Jesus brought in the child Jesus to do for him what the Law required, he took him in his arms and he blessed God."

The focus of this feast is clearly on Jesus. But there are many Marian aspects. It is the mother who carries Jesus into the temple. It is from the arms of his mother that Simeon receives the child Jesus and sings his Nunc Dimittis; it is to Mary that Simeon speaks the prophetic word, "A sword will pierce your own soul too." Mary offers her child in the temple. She will stand at the foot of the cross as Jesus offers himself to the Father. Could Luke see in Mary's offering an adumbration of Jesus' offering of himself? Pope Paul VI explains the significance of this feast:

> The feast of 2 February, which has been given back its ancient name, the Presentation of the Lord, should also be considered as a joint commemoration of the Son and the Mother, if we are fully to appreciate its rich content. It is a celebration of a mystery of salvation accomplished by Christ, a mystery with which the Blessed Virgin was intimately associated as the Mother of the Suffering Servant of Yahweh, as one who performs a mission belonging to ancient Israel, and as model for the new People of God, which is ever being tested in its faith and hope by suffering and persecution. (*To Honor Mary* 9)

℘

Our Lady of Lourdes
Optional Memorial, 11 February

The feast of Our Lady of Lourdes was instituted by Pope St. Pius X in 1907. The apparitions of Our Lady to St. Bernadette—eighteen in all—took place between 11 February and the 16 July 1858.

Our Lady introduced herself to Bernadette with the famous words "I am the Immaculate Conception." This is how Bernadette described her experience:

> The Lady spoke to me a third time and asked me if I was willing to come to her over a period of a fortnight. . . . I went back for fifteen days, and each day the Lady appeared to me, with the exception of a Monday and a Friday. She reminded me again to tell the priests to build a chapel, asked me to wash in the spring, and to pray for sinners. I asked her several times who she was, but she gently smiled at me. Finally, she held her arms outstretched and raised her eyes to heaven and told me that she was the Immaculate Conception. (Office of Readings, 11 February)

Ever since then, millions of pilgrims have made their way to Lourdes and have experienced healing in body, mind, and spirit. At Lourdes Our Lady asked for conversion, for prayers for the conversion of sinners.

ॐ

The Annunciation of the Lord
Solemnity, 25 March

The prayer over the gifts in the Mass for the feast of the Annunciation of the Lord shows clearly the profound significance of this feast. We pray:

> Almighty Father, as we recall the beginning of the Church when your Son became man, may we celebrate with joy today this sacrament of your love.

We are celebrating in this feast the beginning of the church. The church had its beginning when Jesus its head was conceived in Mary's womb. Through the will of God and the yes of Mary, the Son of God became man. Mary's cooperation was needed for the conception and the birth of Jesus; cooperating in the birth of the head she cooperated in the birth of the body.

In focusing on the beginning of the church, the prayer of the Mass opens our minds to what Pope Paul VI called "the ecclesial dimension of devotion to Mary." We cannot and should not think of Mary by herself. In the Scriptures Mary is revealed as the Mother of Jesus, "the woman" at Cana and the foot of the cross, the one who is praying in the midst of the disciples when the Holy Spirit comes. Mary is always in relation to Jesus or in relation to the disciples. Devotion to Mary, therefore, always leads to a deeper relationship to Jesus and the church. As Pope John Paul II said about his own faith journey: "Thanks to Saint Louis of Montfort, I came to understand that true devotion to the Mother of God is actually Christocentric, indeed, it is very profoundly rooted in the mystery of the Blessed Trinity, and the mysteries of the Incarnation and the Redemption."[2] That is why this feast is, in the words of Paul VI, "a joint feast of Christ and the Virgin." In his great encyclical he writes:

> For the solemnity of the Incarnation of the Word, in the Roman calendar the ancient title—the Annunciation of the Lord—has been deliberately restored, but the feast was and is a joint one of Christ and the blessed Virgin: of the Word, who becomes "Son of Mary" (Mk 6:3), and of the Virgin who becomes Mother of God. With regard to Christ, the East and the West, in the inexhaustible riches of their liturgies, celebrate this Solemnity as the commemoration of the salvific "fiat" of the Incarnate Word, who, entering the world, said: "God, here I am! I am coming to obey your will" (cf. Heb 10:7, Ps 39:8-9). They commemorate it as the beginning of the redemption and of the indissoluble and wedded union of the divine nature with the human nature in the one Person of the Word. With regard to Mary, these liturgies celebrate it as a feast of the New Eve, the obedient and faithful virgin, who with her generous "fiat" (cf. Lk. 1:38) became through the working of the Holy Spirit the Mother of God, but also the true Mother of the living, and by receiving into her womb the one Mediator (cf. 1 Tim. 2:5) became the true Ark of the covenant and true Temple of God. These liturgies celebrate it as a culminating moment in the salvific dialogue between

God and man, and a commemoration of the Blessed Virgin's free consent and co-operation in the plan of redemption. *(To Honor Mary* 9)

The Gospel read at the Mass on this feast is Luke 1:26–38, the story of the Annunciation. We remember and celebrate God's request to Mary to be the mother of Jesus and her acceptance, Mary's yes to God's plan of salvation. She agreed to be not just the biological mother of Jesus but the mother of Jesus the Savior, Jesus who would receive the throne of his father David, Jesus the Redeemer. As Cardinal Suenens writes: "To what did she say yes? She said 'yes' to the mystery of the Incarnation. But the incarnation was a redeeming incarnation. Her 'yes' was a 'yes' to that mystery of incarnation and redemption, which are one."[3] This annual celebration of the feast of the Annunciation of the Lord leads the church into an ever deeper reflection on the central mystery of our faith, the mystery of the Son of God becoming man and being carried in Mary's womb.

ॐ

The Visitation of the Blessed Virgin Mary
Feast, 31 May

The church begins the New Year by celebrating the feast of Mary the Mother of God. Halfway through the year she celebrates the visit that Mary made to her cousin Elizabeth carrying within her womb the child Jesus. In this celebration we see Mary on "her pilgrimage of faith," visiting her cousin who has become pregnant with John the Baptist and bringing blessings to her home. Mary brings Emmanuel, God-with-us, into Elizabeth's household. The joy that this presence of the Lord in his mother's womb brings to that household is captured in the first reading, from Zephaniah 3:14–18:

> Shout for joy, daughter of Zion
> Israel, shout aloud!

> Rejoice, exult with all your heart
> daughter of Jerusalem
> The Lord your God is in your midst.

Elizabeth acts on this word. The Gospel, from Luke 1:39–56, tells us that "Elizabeth was filled with the Holy Spirit. She gave a loud cry and said, 'Of all women you are the most blessed. . . . Why should I be honored with a visit from the mother of my Lord?'" Enlightened by the Holy Spirit, Elizabeth recognizes Mary as "the mother of my Lord." She recognizes the reality of what the angel had announced to Mary, namely, "The Holy Spirit will come upon you." The child in Elizabeth's womb, John the Baptist, also recognizes the presence of the Lord. Elizabeth says, "As soon as the sound of your greeting reached my ears the child in my womb leapt for joy." Notice that it was the sound of Mary's voice that brought this grace of Christ to the child in Elizabeth's womb.

The Second Vatican Council sees in the Visitation story a good example of the very close union between Mary and Jesus:

> This union of the mother and the Son in the work of salvation
> is made manifest from the time of Christ's virginal conception
> up to his death: first when Mary, setting out in haste to go to
> visit Elizabeth, was proclaimed blessed by her because of her
> belief in the promise of salvation, and the precursor leaped for
> joy in her womb. (*Lumen Gentium* 57)

The Visitation brings together two expectant mothers. They have much to share with each other because God has done great and surprising things in each of them. Elizabeth, who was barren, had been asking God for years for a child; Mary, who was still very young, was asked by God to have a child. Perhaps the real purpose of Mary's visit was not to help Elizabeth, as has been traditionally thought, but to share the sheer joy of what the Lord was doing in both of them? Who else could really understand what God was doing in Mary, a young pregnant virgin, except Elizabeth, in whom the Lord was also working in a wonderful way? With Elizabeth, Mary could pour out her heart—her joys and fears, her hopes and dreams. And Elizabeth would understand and accept. Tina Beattie captures the significance of the scene at Elizabeth's house:

> In Mary's visit to Elizabeth, we see that pregnant women, treated with such ambivalence in the world of men, are chosen by God as the special bearers of his word. Hannah (1 Samuel), the barren wife, was fertile and creative in the eyes of God. He gave her a new song to sing, a prophecy that would endure until her distant sister Mary took up her song and fulfilled it. God struck dumb the male priest Zechariah and restored the power of speech to pregnant women. The barren Hannah, the elderly Elizabeth and the virgin Mary stand before us, round-bellied and joyful, affirming the restoration of all women in every stage and condition of life to their rightful place in the human community.[4]

The feast of the Visitation celebrates not just a "private visit" of Mary to her cousin, but a public visit, a visit that we know about from divine revelation, which is part of the history of our salvation and belongs to the Gospel of Jesus Christ. We see in this visit a Pentecostal outpouring of the Holy Spirit which enables Elizabeth to proclaim that Mary is "the mother of my Lord," the first profession of faith in both the divinity of Jesus and Mary's divine motherhood. Elizabeth prophetically proclaims "blessed is she who believed." Mary's true blessedness comes from her faith in the promise of God, in the word of God now incarnate in her womb. Elizabeth recognizes this. "The history of faith in the New Testament began with Mary. With Mary the 'mother of faith,' faith began on earth."[5]

The Immaculate Heart of Mary
Optional Memorial

This feast is now celebrated on the day after the feast of the Sacred Heart of Jesus. The opening prayer of the Mass fixes our mind on what God has done for Mary:

Father, you prepared the heart of the Virgin Mary to be a fitting home for your Holy Spirit. By her prayers may we become
a more worthy temple of your glory.

The focus of this feast is on what God has done in the heart of
Mary. St. Augustine prepared the theological ground for this
devotion when he stressed that "long before Mary had conceived
Jesus in her womb she had conceived him in her mind and
heart." Pope John Paul II comments:

> We can say that the mystery of the Redemption took shape
> beneath the heart of the Virgin of Nazareth when she pro-
> nounced her "fiat." From then on, under the special influence
> of the Holy Spirit, this heart, the heart of both a virgin and a
> mother, has always followed the work of her Son and has gone
> out to all those whom Christ has embraced and continues to
> embrace with inexhaustible love. For that reason her heart must
> have the inexhaustibility of a mother. (*Redemptoris mater* 18)

ᙡᎧ

Our Lady of Mount Carmel
Optional Memorial, 16 July

This feast began as a family celebration of the Carmelite Order.
Explaining its presence in the liturgical calendar of the church,
Pope Paul VI wrote:

> Then there are other feasts originally celebrated by particular
> religious families but which today, by reason of the popular-
> ity they have gained, can truly be considered ecclesial, e.g. 16
> July, Our Lady of Mount Carmel. (*To Honor Mary* 22)

ᙡᎧ

Dedication of the Basilica of St. Mary Major
Memorial, 5 August

The basilica of Mary Major in Rome was known as "the mother
church" of Christendom. The first church on this site was built

just after Mary was declared Mother of God (*Theotokos*) by the Council of Ephesus in 431. Following the declaration of Ephesus many churches were dedicated to the Mother of God. Today there are thousands of churches throughout the world dedicated to Mary under one of her many titles.

ℰ

The Assumption of the Blessed Virgin Mary
Solemnity, 15 August

The opening prayer of the Mass of the Assumption makes the theological connections: "In the plan of your wisdom she who bore the Christ in her womb was raised body and soul in glory to be with him in heaven." In celebrating what happened to Mary after her death, the church places before us the christological reason. The Mother of Christ is reunited body and soul with him in heaven. In the preface of the Mass we have placed before us another theological aspect of this feast: "Today the Virgin Mother was taken up into heaven to be the beginning and the pattern of the Church in its perfection and a sign of hope and comfort for your people on their pilgrim way." Christ's redemption, which has now reached its perfection in his mother, will also be perfected in the church. As the Second Vatican Council said, "In the most holy virgin the Church has already reached that perfection whereby she exists without spot or wrinkle" (*Lumen Gentium* 65).

Mary is the perfect disciple. While on earth she was the model disciple as she listened to and lived by the word of God. In heaven she is now the perfect model of what all disciples will become. The Second Vatican Council said:

> In the meantime the mother of Jesus in the glory which she possesses in body and soul in heaven is the image and the beginning of the Church as it is to be perfected in the world to come. Likewise she shines forth on earth, until the day of the Lord shall come (cf. 2 Pet. 3:10), as a sign of certain hope and comfort to the pilgrim People of God. (*Lumen Gentium* 68)

In the liturgy we celebrate that certain hope we have of our final destiny with God. Mary's final destiny in God will also be ours. As Pope Paul VI said:

> It is a feast of her destiny of fullness and blessedness of the glorification of her immaculate soul and her virginal body, of her perfect configuration to the Risen Christ; a feast that sets before the eyes of the Church and of all mankind the image and the consoling proof of the fulfillment of their final hope, namely that this full glorification is the destiny of all those whom Christ has made his brothers and sisters, "having flesh and blood in common with them" (Heb. 2:14). (*To Honor Mary* 6)

The Gospel of the Mass is the story of the Visitation. In her response to the praise of Elizabeth, "Blessed is she who believed that the promise made to her by the Lord would be fulfilled," Mary sang her Magnificat proclaiming, "He who is mighty has done great things for me." Her Immaculate Conception was surely a great thing, the grace of preservative redemption; the incarnation of the Son of God in her womb, the gift of her divine motherhood was a great thing, a totally unmerited grace. Now the final great thing, her glorious Assumption into heaven is the occasion of this feast. The church had to celebrate it. Long before it was a dogma of faith, it was a celebration in the hearts and the liturgy of the faithful. Pope John Paul comments:

> In her exultation Mary confesses that she finds herself in the very heart of this fullness of Christ. She is conscious that the promise made to the fathers, first of all to Abraham and his posterity forever is being fulfilled in herself. She is thus aware that concentrated within herself as Mother of Christ is the whole salvific economy, in which "from age to age" is manifested he who, as God of the Covenant, remembers his mercy. (*Redemptoris mater* 36)

In the light of the Assumption we can surely say a great "Amen" to Mary's words, "He who is mighty has done great things for me." And he will do the same great thing for us. That is why the feast of the Assumption is a source of hope for the church, an assurance of our final destiny with God in heaven.

℘

The Queenship of Mary
Memorial, 22 August

The Second Vatican Council teaches that Mary "was exalted by the Lord as Queen of all in order that she might be more thoroughly conformed to her Son, the Lord of Lords and conqueror of sin and death" (*Lumen Gentium* 59). This feast of the Queenship of Mary, instituted in 1954 by Pope Pius XII and celebrated on 31 May, is now celebrated on the octave of the Assumption. Pope Paul VI gives the reason:

> The solemnity of the Assumption is prolonged in the celebration of the Queenship of the Blessed Virgin Mary, which occurs seven days later. On this day we contemplate her who, seated beside the King of Ages, shines forth as Queen and intercedes as Mother. (*To Honor Mary* 6)

℘

The Birthday of the Blessed Virgin
Feast, 8 September

According to St. Paul Jesus was born "in the fullness of time" (Gal. 4:4). The birth of his mother is, therefore, the dawn of "the fullness of time" and should be celebrated in faith.

The Scriptures tell us nothing about the birth of Mary or about her parents, whom the church honors as Sts. Joachim and Anne. We take these names from the apocryphal writing called the *Protevangelium of James.* This book, which claimed the name of the apostle James, "the brother of the Lord," was never accepted by the church as a historical document, yet it had great influence in the early church. It set out to answer the questions everyone had about Mary, about her birth and childhood, about her parents. While honoring the ancient tradition that identifies Mary's parents as Sts. Joachim and Anne, we must remember with Karl Rahner:

> Beyond what is contained in Scripture, the Church knows nothing of the life of the blessed Virgin, of the external events of which it was made up. No historically trustworthy tradition that might add to Scripture has been preserved in the Church. It is as if all these details were really fundamentally unimportant, and were hidden in God's mystery, so that men might only know the one thing that matters, that is, that Mary is the mother of the Lord.[6]

ॐ

Our Lady of Sorrows
Memorial, 15 September

Michelangelo's famous statue the *Pietà* is the artistic expression for all time of the Christian awareness of Mary's sorrows. The church remembers and celebrates her sufferings the day following the exaltation of the Holy Cross (14 September). The Gospel of the Mass is from Luke 2:33–35, Simeon's prophecy concerning the sword that would pierce her soul. Pope John Paul II sees in these words a "second Annunciation":

> Simeon's words seem like a second Annunciation to Mary for they tell her of the actual historical situation in which her Son is to accomplish his mission, namely in misunderstanding and sorrow. (*Redemptoris mater* 16)

Mary's exalted vocation as Mother of God involved her most intimately in the life of Jesus. She carried him in her womb; she nursed him at her breast; she educated and formed him as a boy; and she followed him on his way to Calvary, as his faithful disciple, standing at the foot of his cross and sharing with him, through her compassion what he suffered in his passion.

༄

Our Lady of the Rosary
Memorial, 7 October

For many centuries the Rosary has been a method of prayer most valued by Catholics of every walk of life. Towering intellectuals and the simplest of souls, extraordinary saints and mystics, and poor, weak, and sinful people have all found in the Rosary a way of communing with God. In the words of Pius XII, the Rosary is "a compendium of the entire Gospel." It is most appropriate, therefore, that the feast of the Rosary, which has been such a means of grace to so many, should be celebrated worldwide in the liturgy of the Catholic Church.

༄

The Presentation of the Blessed Virgin
Memorial, 22 November

The feast of the Presentation of the Blessed Virgin is one of the twelve major feasts of Our Lady in the Eastern church. In the Western church, however, it was a late arrival. This was due to the fact that there is no scriptural basis for the belief that Mary, as a child, lived in the temple in Jerusalem. We owe this legend to the apocryphal *Protevangelium of James,* which was written around the year 150, not too long after the Gospel of John. Its intention was to glorify Mary and to supply details about her parents, her childhood, her marriage to Joseph, and the birth of Jesus. None of these details has any bearing on Christ's work of redemption, the subject of the Gospels, but people were curious and wanted to know such personal and familial stories. Here is how the *Protevangelium of James* satisfied this curiosity:

> The months passed and the child [Mary] grew. When she was two years old, Joachim said to Anna, "Let us bring her up to

the temple of the Lord, so that we may fulfill the promise which we made, lest the Lord send (some evil) upon us and our gift become unacceptable." And Anna replies: "Let us wait until the third year, that the child may then no more long after her father and mother." And Joachim said: "Very well." And when the child was three years old, Joachim said: "Let us call the undefiled daughters of the Hebrews, and let each take a lamp, and let it be burning, in order that the child may not turn back and her heart be enticed away from the temple of the Lord." And he did so until they went up to the temple of the Lord. And the priest took her and kissed her and blessed her, saying: "The Lord has magnified your name among all generations; because of you the Lord at the end of days will manifest his redemption to the children of Israel." And he placed her on the third step of the altar, and the Lord God put grace upon the child, and she danced for joy with her feet, and the whole house of Israel loved her. And her parents went down wondering, praising and glorifying the almighty God because the child did not turn back to them. And Mary was in the temple nurtured like a dove and received food from the hand of an angel. (§§7–8)[7]

Although this delightful story has no historical basis in the Scripture, it is full of theological significance. Mary, from her earliest years, belonged wholly to God. This is the theological truth and the liturgical justification for this feast.

$\wp$

The Immaculate Conception of the Blessed Virgin Mary
Solemnity, 8 December

The truth of our faith that the church celebrates in the feast of the Immaculate Conception is beautifully expressed in the preface of the Mass:

You allowed no stain of Adam's sin
to touch the virgin Mary.

Full of grace she was to be the worthy mother of your Son,
Your sign of favor to the Church at its beginning,
and the promise of its perfection as the bride of
Christ, radiant in beauty.
Purest of virgins, she was to bring forth your Son,
the innocent lamb who takes away our sins.
You chose her from all women to be our advocate
with you and our pattern in holiness.

In this feast the church celebrates two profound truths. First of all, Mary was redeemed in advance so that she could be the worthy mother of the Son of God. Second, in her state of freedom from all sin, we see the beginning of the church of Christ, the dawn of our salvation. The second reading in the Mass, from Ephesians 1:3-6, 11-12 gives us the biblical basis for these truths. Mary was chosen "in Christ before the world was made to be holy and spotless." This word of God from Ephesians, true of the whole church through the grace of redemption, which frees us from sin, was true of Mary before she was conceived, because that same grace of redemption kept her free from sin from the very first moment of her existence.

The church's faith in the Immaculate Conception is often badly misunderstood. The church does not teach that Mary did not need redemption; it teaches, in the words of the defining dogma, that "from the first moment of her conception, by the singular grace and privilege of Almighty God, in view of the merits of Christ Jesus the Savior of the human race, she was preserved immune from all stain of original sin." Mary's redemption took the form of her "preservation from original sin," the creation of her loving relationship with God the Father from the first moment of her life. This was the Father's gift to her, given so that she could be the worthy mother of his Son. It was the Father who saluted Mary, through the angel, with the words "full of grace." God declares that Mary is full of grace. The church, in answering the question, When did she become full of grace? says, "From the first moment of her conception." In answering the question,

How did she become full of grace? the church says, "In view of the merits of Christ Jesus." And in answering the question, Why was Mary full of grace? the church says, Because "she was to be the worthy mother of God's Son."

This "singular grace and privilege" of the Immaculate Conception was given to Mary not for her own glorification but for the sake of her motherhood of Jesus. Motherhood is not simply a biological process. The child is not simply born of the mother's body. The child is equally born of the mother's faith and love. If Mary did not have faith in God the Father of Jesus, if her whole being was not united to God in love, how could the Son of the Father be born of her? How could Mary be alienated from God the Father by sin and at the same time become mother of the Son of God? As Hans Urs von Balthasar rightly says,

> Her freedom from sin is the condition for the Word of God being able to become flesh. This was not first of all a physical affair, but rather it needed a complete agreement, like a spiritual womb, so that God could insert himself into the human community. Mary's entire person, soul and body indivisibly united, was the vessel for his entry.[8]

We have recalled the fifteen special feasts of Our Lady, which the church celebrates annually. There are many other celebrations of the memory of Mary in the liturgy. "The Advent season," as Pope Paul VI noted, "should be considered as a time particularly suited to devotion to the Mother of the Lord" (*To Honor Mary* 4). During Advent, the church is waiting for the coming of the Savior. Mary, as she awaited the birth of Jesus, is our model of how to await the coming Christ. And, as Pope Paul VI said,

> The Christmas Season is a prolonged commemoration of the divine, virginal and salvific Motherhood of her whose "inviolate virginity brought the Savior into the world." In fact, on the Solemnity of the Birth of Christ the Church adores the Savior and venerates his glorious Mother. On the Epiphany, when she celebrates the universal call to salvation, the Church

contemplates the Blessed Virgin, the true Seat of Wisdom and true Mother of the King, who presents to the Wise Men for their adoration the Redeemer of all peoples. On the feast of the Holy Family of Jesus, Mary and Joseph (the Sunday within the octave of Christmas) the Church meditates with profound reverence upon the holy life led in the home at Nazareth by Jesus, the Son of God and the Son of Man, Mary his Mother, and Joseph the just man (cf. Mt 1:19). (*To Honor Mary* 5)

The liturgy, therefore, celebrates Mary's presence in the mystery of Christ and the church throughout the year with special Marian Solemnities, Feasts, and Memorials, as well as in the daily remembrance of Mary in the Mass and seasonal remembrances especially during Advent and Christmas. The Christian consciousness of the Catholic faithful, especially of those who share in the eucharistic celebration every day, is formed through this liturgical spirit and celebration. We could say that the Catholic liturgy is the first school for fostering devotion to Mary and forming in those who participate in the liturgical celebrations a truly Marian attitude and spirituality.

7

Mary in Private Devotion

S PEAKING ABOUT DEVOTION to Our Blessed Lady, the Second Vatican Council said:

> Let the faithful remember moreover that true devotion consists neither in sterile or transitory affection, nor in a certain vain credulity, but proceeds from true faith, by which we are led to recognize the excellence of the Mother of God, and we are moved to a filial love towards our mother and to the imitation of her virtues. (*Lumen Gentium* 67)

Devotion to Mary, as we saw in the last chapter, is highly developed on the liturgical level in the church. Yet it must also be said that the vast majority of people would never participate in the celebration of the Marian liturgical feasts. Most practicing Catholics would certainly be at Mass on New Year's Day when we celebrate the divine motherhood; many would seek to celebrate the Assumption and the Immaculate Conception. But the other feasts would not have much influence on the majority of the church. This means that the Marian piety of the faithful is nourished more by private and paraliturgical devotions than by the actual liturgical devotions of the church. Pilgrimages to Our Lady's shrines and sites of apparitions, public novenas in honor of Our Lady, the Rosary on an individual or group level, the daily recitation of a few Hail Marys—these are the sources for the devotion of the faithful. In this chapter we will look at a few devotions.

✺

Marian Devotion and the Word of God

First let us look at how we can base our devotion to Mary entirely on the word of God. Here are some practical steps as a prayer exercise.

1. Listen to the word of Jesus as he says, "She is your mother." Thank Jesus for this gift of his own mother. Thank him for speaking this word of God and ask him for the grace to live by it. Ask the Holy Spirit to allow the word of Jesus, "She is your mother," to have in your life the meaning that Jesus wants it to have.

2. Recall that Jesus speaks the word of God to his mother: "He/she is your son/daughter." Mary is living by that word, and with a motherly heart she is anxious to be close to you and help you on your way through life. Jesus has entrusted you, through his word from the cross, to his mother. Since Jesus has entrusted you to his mother, can you entrust yourself to her?

3. Accept these life-giving words of Jesus from the cross to his mother and to yourself, "the disciple whom he loves"; accept that on his word and through the power of his Spirit Mary is your spiritual mother; again, through that same creative word of Jesus and the power of the Holy Spirit, you are Mary's spiritual daughter or son.

4. Speak to Mary in your heart, with the words of your heart. Or greet her as the archangel Gabriel and St. Elizabeth did in the Gospel of Luke: "Hail, full of grace, the Lord is with you, blessed are you among women and blessed is the fruit of your womb." You are now seeing Mary through the light of the Gospel. She is full of grace;

she is blessed. Your attitude to her is being formed by the word of the Gospel; you are fulfilling her own prophecy and calling her blessed.

5. Having acknowledged Mary for who she really is, you may want to ask her for her prayers. The church has said this prayer, the second part of the Hail Mary for many centuries: "Holy Mary, Mother of God, pray for us sinners now and at the hour of our death." The church teaches us to honor Mary as holy, while presenting ourselves as sinners in the sure knowledge that Mary, like her Son, loves sinners.

6. You are now in a devotional relationship with Mary. The Holy Spirit will fill your heart with love for Mary. That love will find its own expression. Your personal devotion to Mary may be very different from the devotion of others. Your devotion is a gift of love given to you by the Holy Spirit. With that love in your heart you begin to live by the word of God, "She is your mother."

7. As you become aware of the gift of the Mother of God as your own mother, aware of her love and presence in your life, you will find that your heart will want to say something else to Mary. It will be entirely personal to yourself. St. Aloysius Gonzaga used to repeat with holy amazement, "Mother of God and my mother." Meditation on those simple words will lead you very deep into a faith relationship with Mary.

8. As you begin to pray the Hail Mary you will become aware of so many truths: "the Lord is with you." The angel proclaims that God the Father is with Mary. The Father is with Mary in such a loving, personal way that he invites her, with divine courtesy, to agree to the great miracle of the incarnation of his Son, Jesus Christ. Meditating on God the Father's request to "his lowly handmaid" to become the mother of his Son is always very

fruitful. The Father had such respect, such regard for Mary in her freedom that he sent the archangel Gabriel to her to ask her consent. He didn't command; he invited. And what trust the Father had in Mary!

9. The angel told Mary that she would conceive by the power of the Holy Spirit: "The Holy Spirit will come upon you and the power of the Most High will overshadow you." At the beginning of the creation story in the book of Genesis we are told that God's Spirit hovered over the water" (Gen. 1:1). God's Spirit will "hover over Mary," if she agrees, and there will be a new creation. The Son of God will become a human being, and our fallen nature will be restored. Mary will become the temple on earth of the Holy Spirit.

10. Mary responds, "Let it be done unto me according to your word." And the great miracle of the incarnation takes place. She becomes, through the power of the Spirit, the Mother of God. She bears in her womb the Son of God. God dwells with her and in her. She is truly the "ark of the covenant," the temple of the Holy Spirit, the dwelling place of God.

11. Devotion to Mary always leads to a contemplation of the mystery of the Father, the Son, and the Holy Spirit. We are led to contemplate what the Holy Trinity did in Mary. The Father chose her and requested her consent; the Holy Spirit overshadowed her; the Son became incarnate in her womb as her son. All the beauty we admire and revere in Mary is just a reflection of what the Holy Trinity did in her. She is "Holy Mary" because God the Father is with her; she is the virgin mother because the Holy Spirit overshadowed her; she is the mother of our salvation because Jesus Christ, our Savior, was born of her.

12. Once we begin to meditate on Mary and on her relationship with Jesus her son, we will automatically find our-

selves meditating on the mysteries of the life of Jesus: the mysteries surrounding his conception, his birth, and his childhood; the mysteries of his pubic life, passion, and death, the mysteries of his resurrection, ascension, and outpouring of the Holy Spirit. We will find ourselves "meditating on the mysteries of the Rosary."

℘ð

The Rosary

The Rosary is, in the words of Cardinal Newman "the creed turned into prayer." The mysteries of Christ, which we profess in the creed, become the object of our contemplation as we pray the Rosary. It is Jesus, as he is revealed to us in the Gospel, who becomes our constant companion as we meditate on the mysteries of the Rosary. And we say the Rosary in Mary's company, seeing Jesus as she sees him. This fact led Pope Pius XII to declare that the Rosary is "a compendium of the whole Gospel."

The mysteries of the Rosary follow the proclamation of St. Paul in Philippians:

> Make your own the mind of Christ Jesus:
> Who, being in the form of God,
> did not count equality with God
> something to be grasped.
> But he emptied himself,
> taking the form of a slave,
> becoming as human beings are;
> and being in every way
> like a human being,
> he was humbler yet,
> even to accepting death,
> death on a cross.
> And for this God raised him high,
> and gave him a name
> which is above all other names;

and so all beings
in the heavens, on earth
in the underworld,
should bend the knee in the name of Jesus
and that every tongue should acknowledge
Jesus Christ as Lord
to the glory of God the Father.

This hymn of St. Paul outlines how the Son of God became a human being like us, how he entered into the whole process of becoming human, how he humbly accepted death on the cross, and how God raised him to his right hand in glory through the resurrection. The fifteen mysteries of the Rosary provide the prayer context in which we can contemplate the incarnation, death, and resurrection of Jesus. The mysteries are grouped under three main categories: the Joyful Mysteries, the Sorrowful Mysteries, and the Glorious Mysteries. Under each category there are five mysteries, each explicitly mentioned in the Scripture, except for the last two. The mysteries of the Rosary are as follows:

The Joyful Mysteries
   1. The Annunciation (Luke 1:26–38)
   2. The Visitation (Luke 1:39–56)
   3. The Nativity (Luke 2:1–20)
   4. The Presentation in the Temple (Luke 2:22–40)
   5. The Finding in the Temple (Luke 2:41–52)

The Sorrowful Mysteries
   1. The Agony in the Garden (Luke 22:39–54)
   2. The Scourging (Isa. 53:1–5; John 19:1)
   3. The Crowning with Thorns (Matt. 27:27–31)
   4. The Carrying of the Cross (Luke 23:26–32)
   5. The Crucifixion (John 19:17–37)

The Glorious Mysteries
   1. The Resurrection (John 20)
   2. The Ascension (Acts 1:1–11)
   3. The Descent of the Holy Spirit (Acts 2:1–13)

4. The Assumption of Our Lady into Heaven
5. The Crowning of Our Lady in Heaven (Revelation 12)

These fifteen mysteries provide a Christ-centered focus for the mind as we seek to enter more deeply into the mystery of Christ. We pray each mystery in this way: The Our Father is said first. This opens our heart to the love of the Father and to his kingdom, for whose coming we pray with the words "thy kingdom come." Then we say ten Hail Marys (a decade) as we contemplate the love of the Father and the coming of the kingdom in some aspect of the life of Jesus. We conclude the decade with the Gloria. This "Glory be to the Father and to the Son and to the Holy Spirit" is a fitting response to the mystery of God's love contemplated in one of the mysteries of Jesus. The Joyful Mysteries are said on Mondays and Thursdays; the Sorrowful Mysteries on Tuesdays and Fridays; and the Glorious Mysteries on Sundays, Wednesdays, and Saturdays.

Pope Paul VI gave this very clear explanation of the Rosary:

In the harmonious succession of Hail Marys the Rosary puts before us once more a fundamental mystery of the Gospel— the Incarnation of the Word, contemplated at the decisive moment of the Annunciation to Mary. The Rosary is thus a Gospel prayer, as pastors and scholars like to define it, more today perhaps than in the past.

It has also been more easily seen how the orderly and gradual unfolding of the Rosary reflects the very way in which the Word of God, mercifully entering into human affairs, brought about the Redemption. The Rosary considers in harmonious succession the principal salvific events accomplished in Christ, from his virginal conception and the mysteries of his childhood to the culminating moments of the Passover—the blessed Passion and the glorious Resurrection—and to the effects of this on the infant Church on the day of Pentecost, and on the Virgin Mary when at the end of her earthly life she was assumed body and soul into her heavenly home. It has also been observed that the division of the mysteries of the

Rosary into three parts not only adheres strictly to the chrono-
logical order of the facts but above all reflects the plan of the
original proclamation of the faith and sets forth once more
the mystery of Christ in the very way in which it is seen by
Saint Paul in the celebrated "hymn" of the letter to the Philippians—kenosis, death and exaltation. (*To Honor Mary* 44, 45)

No form of prayer in the Western church has been more
widely used or more consistently encouraged by popes and saints
than the Rosary. Great saints like St. Alphonsus de Liguori and St.
Louis Marie de Montfort spread this devotion wherever they
went. In our own day great spiritual leaders like Mother Teresa
and Pope John Paul II have been noted promoters of the Rosary.
Shortly after his election Pope John Paul said, "The rosary is my
favorite prayer. A marvellous prayer! Marvellous in its simplicity
and in its depths."[1] The genius of the Rosary is that it can be
prayed by the simplest of the faithful and the most profound theologian. When Karl Rahner, one of the greatest theologians of the
twentieth century, was physically too frail to deliver his profound theological lectures, he would introduce the theme of the
lecture with a few words and explain that one of his assistants
would read it. Then he himself would sit quietly, as his lecture
was being read, absorbed in his Rosary.

As a method of prayer the Rosary is at once vocal and con-
templative, repetitive yet always changing. The vocal side of the
Rosary, saying the decade, is really the prelude to the contempla-
tion: as we say the Hail Mary we are focusing on the mystery of
Christ in the Annunciation or crucifixion or resurrection. As the
Methodist theologian Neville Ward wrote,

> It seems hard to believe that one can meditate on a theme
> while mentally repeating certain prayers even though these
> are so thoroughly known that little effort is required. As one
> becomes familiar with the Rosary the prayers gradually recede
> to form a kind of "background music," and the mystery is
> before the mind as though one is looking at a religious picture
> or icon. The balance frequently changes, and the prayers

occupy the foreground of the mind for a time, and this may lead to a form of simple attention to God which is more like contemplation. If one find one's mind being led into a stillness and concentration of this kind it is good to let it happen.[2]

In praying the Rosary we alternate between contemplating the mystery and concentrating on the words. In the Hail Mary we are greeting Mary with the very same words the angel used, "Hail, full of grace, the Lord is with you." We can think of the meaning of that greeting in the context of the mystery. We are also saying, in the words of Elizabeth in the Gospel, "Blessed is the fruit of thy womb, Jesus." Again, as we think about Jesus, the fruit of Mary's womb, in the light of the mystery, our mind and spirit can be lifted up to God in new ways. On the other hand, we may be quite unaware of the words we are saying as we concentrate on the mystery. As we focus, for instance on the crucifixion or the resurrection of Jesus, the words can become just a rhythmic melody while our whole attention is taken up with the Lord, either in his great suffering or his glorious triumph over death.

The Rosary is inspired by the great mysteries of Christ. We begin each decade with Christ's own prayer, bringing our whole being to God the Father, opening our lives to his kingdom and asking his forgiveness for our own sins as we resolve to forgive others. We pray ten Hail Marys as we contemplate Christ in his mysteries or as we reflect on the words of Scripture that are used in this prayer. We conclude each decade with a wonderful prayer of praise of the Holy Trinity. Each decade, then, begins with the invocation and adoration of God the Father, develops with the contemplation of God the Son as we pray the Hail Mary, and concludes with the praise and adoration of the Father, the Son, and the Holy Spirit. The Rosary is a perfect model of Christian prayer, based on the mysteries of Christ, which are contemplated in the company of his mother and, as Pope Paul says, "through the eyes of her who was closest to the Lord" (*To Honor Mary* 47). In the company of Mary and through her eyes, through her faith, we look at the mysteries of her Son's life.

We bring our whole life, all our concerns and hopes, to the Rosary. If you are facing some problem or difficulty, you can place it at the very center of the mystery of the Rosary. My mother, who said the fifteen decades of the Rosary each day, was once deeply hurt by something a close friend said to her. When I phoned her to ask her how she was coping, she said, "It is gone now but it took two rosaries to get rid of it." She brought the hurt to the Rosary, and as she contemplated Christ in his great love and in all his suffering, her own hurt was healed.

The daily or regular praying of the Rosary forms within the mind the habit of contemplating Christ, keeps the mysteries of Christ at the forefront of our imagination, and enables us to offer to God, in union with Christ, all our joys and sorrows. The Rosary is both a contemplative and a healing prayer. The mysteries of Christ become the focus of our contemplation; as we offer our whole life to God in union with Mary, in the context of the mysteries of her Son, we experience peace and healing, forgiveness and reconciliation.

Pope Paul VI, who was a zealous advocate of the Rosary, concluded his exhortation with these words: "The Rosary is an excellent prayer, but the faithful should feel serenely free in its regard. They should be drawn to its calm recitation by its intrinsic appeal" (*To Honor Mary* 55). We are not obliged to say the Rosary. It is not a sin not to say the Rosary. But of all the methods of prayer that have been discovered and developed in the church throughout the centuries, there is none more effective or more enriching than the Rosary.

ℰᴀ

Three Hail Marys

Another great devotion to Mary is the recitation of three Hail Marys each morning and again before retiring at night. This is a short but very Christian act of devotion. The Hail Mary itself, when prayed reflectively, is a trinitarian prayer. It is not about Mary; it is about what the Holy Trinity has done in Mary. Notice what we say: "Hail Mary full of grace, the Lord is with thee." The Lord, God the Father, is with Mary. That is why it is good to be in her company. That is why, too, that she is "full of grace." We then say, "Blessed is the fruit of thy womb, Jesus." Our thoughts immediately move from the Father being with Mary to Jesus being conceived in her womb. And we recall the words of the angel, "The Holy Spirit will come upon you and the power of the Most High will overshadow you." We cannot say the Hail Mary in an intelligent way, thinking about the words, without thinking about what the Holy Trinity has done in Mary. The Hail Mary is a totally trinitarian prayer. In the second part of the prayer we say, "Holy Mary, Mother of God." We confess our faith in the divinity of Jesus each time we say that prayer. We can say, therefore, that the much-loved Hail Mary is a trinitarian and Christian prayer in such a way that only a Christian can say it and mean it. Only one who believes that the Father chose Mary and that the Son was conceived in her womb through the power of the Holy Spirit can say and mean this prayer. That is why the prayer is so effective. In the company of Mary, as we greet her, we think about what the Father, the Son, and the Holy Spirit have done in her life.

Throughout the Christian centuries we have wonderful stories of how even one Hail Mary was enough to save some poor sinner in the hour of need. These stories illustrate the great confidence that God's people always had in the powerful intercession of Mary, a confidence that has been so beautifully enshrined in the prayer we call the Memorare: "Remember O most gracious Virgin Mary that never was it heard of that anyone who fled to thy protection, implored thy help, or sought thy intercession was left unaided."

Pope Paul VI said,

The Church's devotion to the Blessed Virgin is an intrinsic element of Christian worship. The honor which the Church has always and everywhere shown to the Mother of the Lord, from the blessing with which Elizabeth greeted Mary (cf. Lk 1:42–45) right up to the expressions of praise and petition used today, is a very strong witness to the Church's norm of prayer and an invitation to become more deeply conscious of her norm of faith. (*To Honor Mary* 56)

The practice of saying three Hail Mary's each morning and evening in honor of Our Blessed Lady is a wonderful devotion in itself and can become the door to a more profound Christian faith.

ℱℶ

Consecration or Entrustment

Devotees of Mary have been led to "entrust themselves, their whole being" to the powerful care and love of the Mother of God. Pope John Paul II has the words *Totus Tuus* inscribed on his papal coat of arms—*totus tuus*, "entirely yours." As a young man, John Paul consecrated himself, following the teaching of St. Louis de Montfort to the Immaculate Heart of May. This act of consecration, which should more accurately be called and "act of entrustment" is, for St. de Montfort a renewal of one's baptismal consecration. In baptism we are "born again of water and the Holy Spirit." We become children of God, and children too of Mary. As we renew our baptismal commitment to be disciples of Jesus and children of the heavenly Father we can, at the same time, entrust all that commitment, discipleship, and love of God to the powerful care and protection of Mary. Mary brought us Jesus in the first place. It was through her consent that he became a human being in her womb. She still wants to bring us Jesus. That is why, in the instinct of the great saints and in the devotion of the Catholic faithful, when we go to Mary, we know she always takes us to her Son. And when we entrust our commitment to

Christ to her motherly care, or when we consecrate ourselves to her, she takes great care of us. Her voice saying, "Do whatever he tells you," echoes more clearly in our hearts. She is also bringing all our own personal needs to Christ her Son. Many great saints testify that the most peaceful way to bring our own personal needs to God is to offer them all to the Mother of the Lord.

When we entrust ourselves in an act of commitment to Mary, we acknowledge that she is our Mother and that we can depend on her powerful intercession. Mary has a personal relationship with each of us. We are not just one in a billion who call her mother. Pope John Paul II speaks very clearly about this relationship in the following magnificent passage:

> Motherhood always establishes a unique and unrepeatable relationship between two people: between mother and child and between child and mother. Even when the same mother has many children, her personal relationship with each of them is of the very essence of motherhood. . . . It can be said that motherhood "in the order of grace" preserves the analogy with what "in the order of nature" characterizes the union between mother and child. In the light of this fact it becomes easier to understand why in Christ's testament on Golgotha his mother's new motherhood is expressed in the singular, in reference to one man: behold your son.
>
> It can also be said that these same words fully show the reason for the Marian dimension of the life of Christ's disciples. This is true not only of John, who at that hour stood at the foot of the Cross together with his Master's Mother, but it is also true of every disciple of Christ, every Christian. The Redeemer entrusts his mother to the disciple, and at the same time he gives her to him as his mother. Mary's motherhood which becomes man's inheritance is a gift: a gift which Christ himself makes personally to each individual. (*Redemptoris mater* 45)

Since Jesus entrusted each of us to the love and care of his Mother, we can practice no better devotion than to freely and gratefully entrust ourselves to Mary our Mother. In a very formal way Pope John Paul II, in union with all the bishops of the Catholic Church, entrusted the whole world to the Immaculate Heart of Mary on 25 March 1984. That was a solemn act of the whole church. When we entrust ourselves to Mary, in a personal act of commitment, dedication, or consecration we are certainly acting within the spirit of what the pope and the bishops did in 1984.

On a priests' retreat years ago I was given this prayer to Our Lady, which I have said each morning ever since:

> Most Holy Virgin Mary, perfect disciple of Jesus, I come to dedicate my life and my priestly ministry to your Immaculate Heart. I desire to abandon myself to the will of Jesus, your Son, and walk in faith with you, my Mother. To you I consecrate my life in the priesthood. I give you every gift I possess of nature and of grace, my body and soul, all that I own and everything I do. Pray for me, that the Holy Spirit may visit me with his many gifts. Pray with me, that by faith I may know the power of Christ and by love make him present in the world. Amen.

The great saints were always convinced that when the Holy Spirit found devotion to Mary in a person's heart he was lavish with his graces. Asking Our Lady to intercede with the Spirit for us is surely a very biblical prayer. Mary was in the midst of the disciples praying for the outpouring of the Spirit on that first Pentecost day. She has a unique relationship with the Holy Spirit. Through this unique relationship the Son of God was born into this world as a human being; through this unique relationship the Son of God is born again in the hearts of those who turn to the Spirit through the intercession of Mary. We learn from Mary how to be open to the Spirit; we need her intercession to dismantle all those barriers we erect to the leading of the Spirit. A daily act of entrusting oneself and all one's needs and cares to Our Blessed Lady is a very good devotion to practice. The act of commitment can be very short: *Totus tuus,* wholly yours, as Pope John Paul has on his papal coat of arms.

꧁

Devotional Reading

In 1750 St. Alphonsus de Liguori published his *Glories of Mary*, a book that has had an enormous influence on the devotional life of Catholics. In his introduction he tells us why he wrote this book: "My wish is to provide the faithful—at slight expense and little effort on their part—with reading matter that will inflame them with love for Mary and at the same time to provide priests with the material needed to foster devotion to this Divine Mother." The fact that new editions of the book are still being published in many languages is proof that Alphonsus realized his goal. In the words of Frederick Jones, his recent biographer, "There must be something remarkable in a work which, within 200 years of its first publication, has been translated into over eighty different languages and appeared in 800 known editions."[3] Alphonsus took a well-known prayer, the Salve Regina (Hail Holy Queen) and with consummate theological and literary skill he produced his masterpiece of Marian literature. He tells us modestly:

> I have left the description of Mary's other qualities to other writers and have dealt mainly with her mercy and her powerful intercession, using the theme of the *Salve Regina,* the great prayer approved by the Church and which she has ordered all the regular and secular clergy to recite during most of the year. Mary's mercy and power are admirably described in it and this is why I have started explaining point by point, this most devout prayer. Besides this, I thought it would please those devoted to our Divine Mother to also enjoy readings, or some discourses, on her principal feasts and her virtues. I bring this book to a close by treating the most commonly used devotional practices which are fully approved by the Church. (Introduction)

No book on Mary has been so widely distributed or so deeply appreciated as the *Glories of Mary*. In the last two centuries millions of Catholics have read this book, many reading a chapter a day. O'Donovon Rossa, a famous Irish political prisoner in the nineteenth century, was moved to tears as he read the *Glories of Mary* in a British jail. Saints and scholars, learned and unlearned alike, have all found comfort and encouragement in this Marian classic. Alphonsus wanted the faithful to read the very best literature on Mary. That is why he worked for over twenty years gathering the material for his book. It is a work of immense scholarship and devotion. As Frederick Jones says,

> Beneath the apparently devotional form of *The Glories of Mary* lies a rich mine of sound theological teaching on the Mother of God. As a positive contribution to the Mariological section of theology, it marked a decisive stage in the doctrinal evolution of the doctrine of Our Lady's Immaculate Conception.[4]

Hamish Swanston, an Alphonsian scholar, helps us to appreciate the *Glories of Mary* by the following comment, which he kindly wrote for me:

> Those who first heard the Saturday sermons from which Alfonso derived the chapters of his book, and those who first read what he himself terms "this most useful book," probably reacted in just the same way as modern hearers and readers react:
>
> 1. Readers had in their hands a perfectly structured book—a reader always knows just where he is: Alfonso offers
>   a) an instruction demonstrating clearly the meaning and implications of giving Mary a particular title or of celebrating a particular feast in her honour, demonstrating too how this meaning fits with other titles and feasts and with the body of Christian teaching;
>   b) a prompting to prayer, both by references to the grand tradition of doctrine and devotion and living expressed in his wide reading of saints' works and Lives, and by Alfonso's own catching enthusiasm for the Lady;

    c) a story which illustrates the effective truth of the doctrine expressed in title or feast, and the effective mediation of the Lady.

2. I like the stories best—as does every decent judge, because
    a) there is an appeal to the imagination in harness with the appeal to doctrine and prayer,
    b) these stories are always about the Lady's doing the job appointed to her on Calvary—she is always handing on to her adopted sons that mercy won for us by Jesus' undergoing the demand of his Father's justice,
    c) this mercy is always shown to be won for every one of us and is always being handed on to scallywags, to highwaymen and prostitutes. There is in this a declaration of the copiousness of redemptive power and love. Thrilling and comforting,
    d) the stories are gathered from all sorts and classes of source literature—patristic, mediaeval, treatises, modern wonders, country wives' tales—so, as they read or listen, "the rough and the educated together," as Alfonso described his congregations at mission services, hear one another's stories: the peasant is told that the bambino (baby Jesus) is like the infant Hercules, the school dominie learns to appreciate the alewife's witness to Mary in the cottage, sitting to hear a poor woman's confession.

Alfonso is thus creating a community as he tells the story, a community of fellow feeling, fellow imagining, across class and money and clan barriers.

    e) The original hearers were no more superstitious or gullible than any one at any other time; we make a great mistake if we think we can do without such stories, and as great a mistake if we think that we have critical instruments to gut them. We cannot do without Cinderella's story in our nursery's program, and we make a fundamental error if we suppose that the story is about a teenager's getting into a mess because she doesn't watch the clock when she's told.

The Neapolitans in the eighteenth century were telling each other the stories collected by Giambattista Basile. They knew all about the "literary genres"—though perhaps they would not have expressed themselves in such terms. They knew that the meaning of Mary's mediation of that mercy won by her Son for them was being presented to them in ways that would stay with them, in their imaginations, for a long while. Just as a modern congregation takes the meaning of these stories now when I retell them of a Sunday morning at Kinnoull.

Alphonsus's *Glories of Mary* fuses the learning of a great scholar with the love of a great saint. We find this same combination of learning and great love in that other great book *The True Devotion* written St. Louis de Monfort. He died in 1716, but his book was not discovered until 1842. Yet, in the past 150 years, this remarkable book has been translated into twenty languages and been published in over three hundred editions.[5] As a young man, Pope John Paul II read the *True Devotion* every day. In the past two hundred years the devout reading of the *Glories of Mary* and the *True Devotion* has played a significant role in the formation of Marian piety in the church. The reading of Marian literature, especially those inspired by New Testament and the Liturgy of the church, such as the great encyclicals of Pope Paul VI and Pope John Paul II, which I have quoted throughout this book, is still a sure source for fostering true devotion to the Mother of God.

৪৯

Novenas

Novenas are a very popular form of devotion to Our Lady. The best known novena worldwide is the novena in honor of Our Lady of Perpetual Help. The beautiful icon with the title Mother of Perpetual Help was given to the Redemptorists by Pope Pius IX in 1865 with the mandate: "*Make her known throughout the world."* At that time the Redemptorist Congregation was spreading throughout the world and wherever they went they brought with them the icon and devotion to Our Lady under the title Our Mother of Perpetual Help. In the icon Mary holds the child Jesus on her left arm and looks out tenderly at us while the long fingers of her right hand point to Jesus. The baby Jesus is clutching the right hand of his mother while he looks steadfastly at the archangel Gabriel, who is holding the cross and the nails. The archangel Michael is also in the icon holding the lance and the pole with the sponge and the vessel containing the vinegar. The focal point of the icon is the hands of Jesus holding the right hand of his mother while he looks steadfastly at the cross. As we contemplate the icon we get the distinct impression that through the cross Mary has the power to help her Son—and to help all her sons and daughters. By clutching her right hand Jesus is endowing her with this power to help, the power that comes from the cross on which he is gazing in the archangel Gabriel's hand. That power of helping is always with Mary—hence her title. She is the Mother of Perpetual Help.

Devotion to the Mother of Perpetual Help spread throughout the world. Hundreds of churches bear this title; dioceses have chosen Mary under this title as their patroness; new religious congregations of sisters have chosen Our Lady of Perpetual Help for their title; in thousands of parishes throughout the Catholic world priests have special devotions to the Mother of Perpetual Help. In Britain, Ireland, the United States, and Canada, the novena to Our Mother of Perpetual Help reached its peak in the 1950s and 1960s. Since then there has been a great decline in the numbers making the weekly novena. But devotion to Our Mother of Perpetual Help has revived in a new form. In many places in Ireland and Britain, parishes have "the nine days prayer" or the "Solemn Novena" in honor of Our Mother of Perpetual Help. We will listen to Fr. Tim Buckley describing his experience preaching the Solemn Novena to Our Lady of Perpetual Help in the Redemptorist church in Belfast:

From Wednesday June 17 to Thursday June 25 1998 I was privileged to be one of the team of preachers for the Solemn
Novena in honour of Our Lady of Perpetual Help at Clonard
Monastery in Belfast. While I had heard many accounts of the
extraordinary nature of this annual event, which attracts
crowds of over 15,000 each day, nothing could have prepared
me for the quite overwhelmingly moving experience 'of the
event itself. The vast majority of those who take part are
Roman Catholics, but it was heartening to see that people of
all ages and from across the political and religious divide
attend. They pack the church, surrounding monastery corri-
dors and garden for the ten sessions, beginning at 7:30 in the
morning and ending in candlelight just before midnight. In an
extraordinary operation with back-up teams of priests and
people, ministering the Eucharist and available for counselling
and the Sacrament of Reconciliation, supported by an army of
volunteers stewarding each session.

As the Novena unfolded I tried to identify the key factors
which were having such an enormous effect on me. Two
emerged strongly. Firstly I was touched by the fact that the
prayer of faith of this community was expressed in such a
down-to-earth and practical way. The preaching was direct and
immediate: it touched into the lives of a people who have suffered so much in recent years, but whose hope seemed almost
tangible. Their response was to pour out their prayers in petitions that sometimes reminded me of the openness and forth-
rightness of the Old Testament prophets and psalmists,
pleading with God to be with them and to save them.

Secondly I was struck that once again it was Mary who was
the catalyst for this remarkable demonstration of faith. I say
"once again" because the only comparable experience I could
think of was that of Lourdes. There too Mary is the cause of
thousands of people gathering to present to God their prayers
for healing and strength. In this secular society these shrines
and centres of devotion provide havens where it is the done
thing for people to be seen praying and celebrating their faith,
and where the social order is **supplanted** by the gospel order.
By contrast, here the poor, the sick, the handicapped, those in

distress of any kind take centre stage: here we can get a glimpse of what Jesus means when he teaches us the *beatitudes* and tells us that *that last shall be first.*

I experienced during the days of the novena a profound sense of what it means to be part of the family of faith, united in prayer with one another, as well as with those who have gone before us—the communion of saints in heaven—and above all with Mary, the mother of the family.

The novena to Our Lady of Perpetual Help is celebrated each week in thousands of parishes around the world. In the Redemptorist parish in Manila over one hundred thousand people attend the novena services each week. The first service takes place at 6:00 A.M. and is repeated on the hour throughout the day until late at night. In the Redemptorist parish in Singapore around forty thousand people attend the novena each week. The novena is such a popular event in that great city that when the metro system was installed the station next to the church was called novena. But, while the weekly novena is flourishing in some parts of the world, we have to recognize too that in many places it has lost its attraction. Cultural changes in many societies deter people from making weekly commitments. The generation that was "brought up on" novenas and similar devotions to Mary is no longer with us. Yet, while the weekly novena service has diminished, there is an extraordinary attendance at special Solemn Novenas, or Nine Days Prayer, as they are often called, when these are available to people. Hundreds of thousands of people will attend such Solemn Novenas, the kind that Fr. Buckley described above. There is a pastoral lesson in this for the church. People welcome the opportunity to pray for the needs of their families and their personal needs; they need the support of the community of faith in bringing their needs confidently to God; they need to experience the atmosphere of faith and expectation that a good spiritual event creates. A Nine Days Prayer event provides them with that opportunity—it is not a long-term commitment but, at the same time, it is long enough to give people the religious sense that they are involved in real community prayer and spiritual renewal.

ℬↄ

Apparitions and Pilgrimages

Pilgrimages to Marian shrines and places where Our Lady is said to have appeared provide millions of people each year with a vital source of devotion to Our Lady and a renewal in their faith. John Eade gave us some statistics about shrines and numbers of pilgrims:

> The last forty years have seen a vast increase in the numbers of Christian pilgrims. They travel to shrines dotted about Europe, the Americas, Africa and South Asia. Some of the international shrines are visited by several millions of pilgrims in a year—more than four million to Lourdes, five million to Medjugorje, between three to four million each to Czestochowa and Fatima, many again to Guadalupe and Our Lady of the Snows in the Americas. A recent survey of Christian pilgrimages throughout the world identified about 8,500 active shrines.[6]

These statistics of both the number of "active shrines" and the numbers of pilgrims are overwhelming. Nearly all the shrines are shrines of Our Lady and most of the pilgrims are Catholic or Orthodox, though large numbers from other churches and even from no church or religion also visit Mary's shrines. Some of the apparition shrines are known throughout the world: Guadalupe in Mexico, Lourdes in France, Fatima in Portugal, Knock in Ireland, Banneux in Belgium, and Medjugorje in Bosnia-Herzegovina. Our Lady is alleged to have appeared in hundreds of different places in our own time.

What is the point of all these apparitions? Do they produce any lasting fruit in the church and in the lives of people? The only way to respond to these questions is on the pragmatic level:

What is happening there now as a result of the alleged apparition? Each summer, when I am on holiday at home in Ireland, I
go with members of my family to Knock in the West of Ireland,
where Our Lady appeared in 1878. Our spiritual routine is to say
the Rosary, to celebrate the sacrament of Reconciliation, to join
in making the Way of the Cross, and to participate in the Mass
for the pilgrims and the procession of the Blessed Sacrament after
the Mass. Last August (1998), when we were there I presided at
the concelebrated Mass with thousands of pilgrims, on the his-
toric occasion when a bishop of the Church of Ireland (Anglican
Communion) preached. Afterwards my reflection on the day was
as follows: I had spent a very peaceful day in prayer at the beautiful shrine of Our Lady; I had celebrated the sacrament of Reconciliation and shared in a beautiful celebration of the Eucharist;
I had said the Rosary and had taken part in a procession of the
Blessed Sacrament. Furthermore, I had witnessed an ecumenical
step of great significance, namely, a non-Catholic bishop being
welcomed to Our Lady's shrine as the special preacher of the day.
If I applied to what is happening in Knock a hundred and twenty
years after the apparition the rule for discernment given us by
Jesus—namely, "By their fruits you shall know them"—I would
have to say that Knock is a place of excellent fruit, a place of
prayer, worship, reconciliation, and peace.

In 1988 I conducted a year-end retreat for about three hundred young people in London. They prayed with great fervor
through the retreat, welcoming in the New Year with an all-night
vigil before the Blessed Sacrament exposed. During that vigil
many of them gave witness to extraordinary conversions they
experienced at Medjugorje. Some young men related how they
went to Medjugorje just because they wanted to be with their girl-
friends, without any faith or interest in God and no knowledge at
all of Christ, and how they came back with deep Christian faith
and commitment to Christ. The following summer I made my
first visit with a friend to Medjugorje and I experienced for
myself the atmosphere in which those remarkable conversions
took place. Thousands of people, many of them teenagers or in

their twenties, were spending hours in prayer each day. We waited in line with thousands for our turn to go to the sacrament of Reconciliation (there must have been a hundred priests hearing confession that day); we spent three hours in the evening saying the fifteen decades of the Rosary and sharing the Eucharist; we climbed the mountain where the first apparition took place and joined in the prayer meeting; wherever we went, during those days, we found ourselves saying the Rosary together. Where did this very good spirit come from? What instills in people the desire for the sacraments of Reconciliation and the Holy Eucharist? Where does the extraordinary energy for prayer come from? Again, if I judge what is happening in Medjugorje by the Gospel norm, "By their fruit you will know them," I would have to say that something very good indeed is taking place there.

Pilgrims to any of the shrines where Our Lady is said to have appeared will have experienced the spiritual fruits of her presence. She always invites us to deeper faith through conversion and repentance, through prayer and fasting. Marian shrines are, first of all, places where we meet Christ in a new way; places for the celebration of the sacraments of Christ—the Eucharist, Reconciliation, the Anointing of the Sick. Mary herself is never at the center of the pilgrims' attention. She never calls people to herself, she calls them to return to God and to open their lives to Jesus.

Marian shrines today are places of profound evangelization, where pilgrims are challenged to take stock of the whole direction of their lives, to hear again Christ's call to repentance and discipleship, and to receive afresh the great gift of faith. Mary is always bringing the needs of her children to Christ: "they have no wine," "they have no peace," "they have no faith." At her shrines the pilgrim is assured that Mary is interceding for her children. But she is also giving them very specific directions. To each pilgrim she says, "Do whatever he tells you." We don't go on pilgrimage to Mary's shrines to escape from the commands of Christ; we go to be more faithful to his commands. And Mary, who certainly brings our needs before her Son brings his commands clearly to our minds. She is always the evangelist of her Son. Her most astounding work of evangelization took place at Guadalupe in Mexico. On 9 December 1531, Juan Diego, an Aztec Indian in Mexico, was on his way to Mass. Our Lady, dressed as a young, pregnant Aztec woman, appeared to him. She told him that she was the Mother of God and she asked him to go to the bishop and tell the bishop that she wanted a church built on the place where she stood. On his first encounter with the bishop Juan Diego didn't get very far. Naturally the bishop was very cautious. He asked that the Lady give him a sign. He asked for roses. Juan Diego knew that roses didn't grow or bloom in the middle of winter but, nevertheless, he told the Lady that that was what the bishop wanted. She told him to go up the hill and pick the roses. Juan Diego, to his amazement, found beautiful roses in the snow. He gathered the roses and the Lady arranged them in his cloak and he took them to the bishop. As he placed the roses before the bishop, he was amazed to see the bishop and those with him fall to their knees in veneration. Then he saw on his cloak the perfect image of the Lady he had seen on the hill. The bishop arranged for the image to be taken to a small hut on the hill where it remained until a church could be built. During the next seven years over eight million Aztec Indians were converted to Christ and baptized. That is the most extraordinary story of evangelization of any people in the history of the church. Our Lady intervened in the difficult circumstances of the Aztec people. They had been defeated by the invading Spaniards and shamelessly abused and deprived of their human dignity; they were victims of a pagan religion whose god demanded human sacrifice. Mary came to them as their mother, and through her presence she brought them the light of Christ.

Apparitions have to be discerned. The fact that a group of people claim to have seen a beautiful woman whom they identify as Mary is no reason at all for believing that they have really seen the Blessed Virgin. The bishop of the diocese where the alleged apparition takes place normally sets up a commission of qualified experts to study the phenomena surrounding the apparition: the story of the visionaries, the miracles that are being claimed, such as miracles of healing; the testimony of the lives of the visionaries (Are they credible witnesses? Are they prone to hallucinations?); the messages of the apparition (Are they in conformity with the Gospel and the teaching of the church?). The bishop has many questions he must ask and answer satisfactorily before he is in a position to make any judgment. When he finally reaches his decision he has, as Frederick Jelly points out, three options. He may decide that: (1) the alleged apparitions show all the signs of being authentic or a truly miraculous intervention from heaven; (2) the presumed apparition is clearly not miraculous or there are not sufficient signs manifesting it to be so; or (3) it is not evident whether or not the alleged apparition is authentic. "In principle," Fr. Jelly notes, "the first two verdicts close the case—declaring it either authentic or not. The third possibility keeps the case open, implying that it could be many years before a final judgement may be made or it falls into oblivion."[7]

Even when the church approves of an apparition, no Catholic has to believe that such an apparition really took place. Apparitions are not part of Catholic faith; we don't profess our belief in apparitions.

8

Mary at the Millennium

A S THE CHURCH ENTERS THE THIRD MILLENNIUM, it is still singing Mary's song and fulfilling Mary's prophecy. Two thousand years ago Mary foretold that all generations would call her blessed. Countless Christians throughout the ages and in the world today have shown by their lives and devotion to Mary that this prophecy was true, a true word from God. In the third millennium of the year of Our Lord, each new generation will join their voices to the past generations and call Mary "blessed." We have the privilege of belonging to the first generation of the third millennium, which will fulfill Mary's prophecy and continue to call her "blessed." We could do no better than to take Mary's song, her Magnificat, and make it our own. Our spirituality in the new millennium should be Marian, echoing her song of trust in the future. It is a prophetic song of liberation and trust, a heartfelt song of gratitude and praise, a song for the new millennium.

ℰ

Mary's Spirituality

Mary's spirituality, that is, the way she saw her relationship with God and how she lived it, is memorably expressed in the opening verse of her Magnificat: "My soul proclaims the greatness of the Lord and my spirit exults in God my savior." These magnificent words have thrilled the hearts of Christians in every generation. The simplicity, the depth, the fervor of her Magnificat, the first song of the church, gave the tune for all succeeding generations. Mary doesn't say, "I magnify"; she says, "my soul magnifies" and "my spirit exults." She is emphasizing her total involvement in this act of praise: her whole being is involved. As befits one who "ponders in her heart," the Magnificat is a deeply pondered, consciously chosen, joyfully delivered song of praise and gratitude. It is Mary's considered response to the Annunciation. This is how St. Luke introduces it (1:46–48):

> And Mary said:
> My soul proclaims the greatness of the Lord
> and my spirit exults in God my saviour
> because he has looked upon the humiliation of his servant.
> Yes, from now onwards all generations will call me blessed.

The Magnificat contains in itself a complete profession of Mary's faith: her faith in the God of the promises; her faith in her Son in whom the promises are fulfilled; her faith in divine justice, which will restore God's order of creation and save the poor; her confidence that her people, Israel, will be saved.

The Magnificat, attributed by St. Luke to the Mother of Christ, and sung for centuries each day by the church at Evening Prayer, develops in three stages. The first stage concerns Mary herself and her deep faith in the God of her salvation; the second stage praises the God of justice, who liberates the poor and the oppressed; the third stage concerns her people Israel, God's people, who will receive the mercy of God.

The church accepts that the Magnificat, composed under the influence of the Holy Spirit, is God's word to us, revealing the innermost thoughts and feelings of the Mother of God as she reflected on the wonderful mystery of the incarnate Son of God whom she was carrying in her womb. Scholars discuss in great depth the literary composition of the Magnificat. Did Mary spontaneously compose this song herself? Was it composed in the early Jewish-Christian church and later attributed to Mary by St. Luke? Was it a Jewish battle hymn adapted by St. Luke? These are fascinating questions that deserve study in their own right.[1] In this chapter, however, we will not be discussing any of these historical and literary questions concerning the composition of the Magnificat. Rather we will be accepting the Magnificat, as the church does each day in the Evening Prayer, as Mary's song of praise and thanksgiving. The Magnificat is a life-giving word of God to us. It is the source and the pattern for true praise of God. We can make our own the prayer that Martin Luther addressed to Mary before he began his commentary on the Magnificat: "May the tender Mother of God herself procure for me the spirit of wisdom thoroughly to expound this song of hers."[2]

Before we consider the various parts of the Magnificat, let us look at its exact context. Why did Mary start singing? Notice that St. Luke introduces her song with the words "And Mary said . . . ." The context of the Magnificat is the Visitation. It is Mary's response to what Elizabeth said. This is how St. Luke describes the scene:

> Mary set out at that time and went as quickly as she could into the hill country to a town in Judah. She went into Zechariah's house and greeted Elizabeth. Now it happened that as soon as Elizabeth heard Mary's greeting, the child leapt in her womb and Elizabeth was filled with the Holy Spirit. She gave a loud cry and said, "Of all women you are the most blessed, and blessed is the fruit of your womb. Why should I be honored with a visit from the mother of my Lord? For the moment your greeting reached my ears, the child in my womb leapt for joy. Yes, blessed is she who believed that the promise made her by the Lord would be fulfilled." (Luke 1:39–45)

Mary's entrance into Zechariah's house has a Pentecostal impact: the child in Elizabeth's womb leaps for joy; Elizabeth herself is filled with the Holy Spirit and acknowledges the divine maternity of Mary, "the Mother of my Lord." St. Paul says that "nobody is able to say, 'Jesus is Lord' except in the Holy Spirit" (1 Cor. 12:3). Elizabeth was so under the influence of the Holy Spirit that she proclaimed that Mary's son was Lord before he was born and she gave her cousin the wonderful title of "the Mother of my Lord." Elizabeth didn't simply see her young cousin paying her a social visit. In the Holy Spirit she saw "the Mother of my Lord" visiting her and occasioning extraordinary grace by her very presence: "as soon as your greeting reached my ears the child in my womb leapt for joy." John the Baptist in his mother's womb was touched by Mary's Spirit-filled greeting. And notice that it was "at the sound of Mary's voice." Mary mediated this extraordinary grace to the Baptist because her voice was the voice of the Mother of the Baptist's Lord, the Mother of his Savior. Catharina Halkes comments:

> What always strikes me in particular here is that it was precisely in the encounter of two women, both playing a role in salvation history, each of them pregnant with prophetic life, that the spark of the Spirit flashed over. Mary too was taken out of herself, the child moved in her womb, and all this produced the climate of Mary's prophetic vision.[3]

Elizabeth's praise of Mary and her acknowledgment that she is "the Mother of my Lord" make it quite clear that the Holy Spirit has revealed to her what has happened at the Annunciation. She proclaims Mary blessed "because she believed," and we can suppose that her recognition confirmed Mary in her own faith. Mary saw that the Holy Spirit who had overshadowed her at the Annunciation had revealed to Elizabeth the mystery of the incarnation. Elizabeth already recognized that the baby in her womb was the source of this grace. It was not Mary as cousin, but Mary as "the Mother of my Lord." With Elizabeth's confession of her son as "my Lord" and her acknowledgment of Mary's faith, Mary can now respond. And what a God-centered response she gave.

Before we look at her response we must remind ourselves once again of the purpose St. Luke had in mind when writing his Gospel: "I, in my turn, after carefully going over the whole story from the beginning, have decided to write an ordered account for you, Theophilus, so that your Excellency may learn how well founded the teaching is that you have received" (Luke 1:3). Every line of his book serves his evangelistic purpose of demonstrating the truth of the Gospel. By placing the Magnificat on Mary's lips, Luke can demonstrate her deep faith in the incarnation, in the promises of God, in God's fidelity, in his special love for the poor. Luke's narrative, breathing the spirit of the Old Testament promises, has a theological purpose throughout, namely, to focus

on Jesus as Messiah and Lord, the one in whom all the promises
of God are fulfilled.

As Mary looks into the depth of the mystery of God, she recognizes herself in her true relationship with God. The immediate
source of her joy is "because he has looked upon his lowly handmaid." Elizabeth has proclaimed Mary's great dignity. She is "the
Mother of my Lord." In response, Mary recognizes her true lowliness in the presence of God. She is the slave, the handmaid of
the Lord. That she is the Mother of the Lord is God's choice for
her; that she is the handmaid of the Lord is Mary's choice for herself. Her choice to be handmaid manifests her total consecration
to God. Her whole life is dedicated to his service. Being the Lord's
handmaid, his slave, constitutes Mary's very identity. God saw
her as *kecharitōmenē,* full of grace, the one transformed by grace.
She saw herself as the Lord's slave, as the one who depended
entirely on her Lord. Mary, without denying or qualifying God's
view of her, declares her own view of herself: the handmaid, the
servant of the Lord. To one who says that Mary must have had a
poor image of herself if she saw herself simply as a handmaid or
a slave, we can only reply by saying, "handmaid to whom?"
Handmaid to God, the Creator of all, in service to God for the salvation of the human race. We can see in Mary a wonderful grace
of self-acceptance, a liberating acknowledgment of her true dignity as she depended on God for her whole being and for the reason for her existence. Mary fully accepted herself because she
knew and lived her relationship with God.

In applying to herself the title "handmaid or servant of the
Lord," Mary shows us how she sees and feels about herself. Total
human fulfillment is found not in asserting one's freedom to be
independent of God but in using one's freedom to choose to be
God's servant. In Mary's mind there is no conflict between freedom and obedience. Indeed, the only way to safeguard one's freedom is through joyful obedience to God, who is the source of
our freedom. In her freedom Mary makes her fundamental
option for God—God first and last, God before all things and God
in and through all things.

In response to Elizabeth, Mary can say, "He has looked on

his lowly handmaid. Yes, from this day forward all generations will call me blessed." Elizabeth, under the influence of the Holy Spirit, is the first to call Mary blessed. Each generation will continue to do what Elizabeth has begun. Mary carefully explains why all generations will call her blessed: "because God has looked upon his lowly handmaid." Martin Luther, in his excellent book on the Magnificat, focuses on God's action of "regarding" or "looking at" Mary. He writes:

> Mary confesses that the foremost work God wrought for her was that he regarded her, which is indeed the greatest of his works, on which all the rest depend and from which they all derive. For where it comes to pass that God turns his face towards one to regard him, there is naught but grace and salvation, and all the gifts and works must needs follow.[4]

The Magnificat was composed not just in the light of the Annunciation and Elizabeth's praise, but in the light of the whole mystery of Jesus—his birth, life, public mission, death and resurrection, and the outpouring of the Holy Spirit at Pentecost. When the early Christians heard it sung, they understood exactly its meaning. We can be sure that this song was sung long before Luke wrote it down. This means, of course, that already in the second or third generation of the faith Christians held Mary in very high esteem: she was hailed as "the Mother of the Lord"; it was taken for granted "that all generations called her blessed." It would be most unlikely that St. Luke would write down this prophecy if his own community was not already fulfilling it. Mary's prophecy, being a word of God, will be fulfilled. As Martin Luther put it: "The Virgin Mary means to say simply that her praise will be sung from one generation to the another, so that there will never be a time when she shall not be praised."[5]

Isidro Goma Civit writes:

> By the time the definitive redactor set down in writing the Gospel of the Infancy, this prediction of Mary's could already be witnessed in the Church. The "generation" or "generations" of communities for whom Luke was writing could feel themselves included in it. The words of the Magnificat when

they came to be written down were prophecy in view of the centuries to follow, but they were already history for the decades of Christian life already passed.[6]

Mary rejoices because God looks on her lowly state. She does not depend on herself—on her social situation or on her wealth. She relies solely on God. In this total dependence Mary is the face of the church throughout the ages—a humble virgin, with no power or influence but totally dependent on God. When the church fails to show this Marian face to the world, when the church enters into coalition with the powers of this world, she always suffers. The church, like Mary, must only "rejoice in God my Savior." Vatican II says, "Mary stands out among the humble and the poor of the Lord who confidently hope in him for salvation and receive it from him" (*Lumen Gentium* 55). Civit comments:

> Mary is both the face and the heart of a people who cannot count on the power of this world's rulers but only on that of God. Her Magnificat is the hymn of the poor, the "every-day song" for the Church. But if anyone dares to sing it while refusing to accept humility of heart, he condemns himself.[7]

ॐ

The Spirituality of Praise

Mary's spirituality is one of praise and thanksgiving rooted in the awareness of her lowliness. Before God she has nothing that she has not received—she has no merit of her own, no grace of her own, no wisdom of her own. She is humble of heart. It would not be an exaggeration to say that Jesus, who says "learn from me because I am meek and humble of heart" learned and acquired these virtues from his mother. We could also say that long before Jesus proclaimed "How blessed are the poor in spirit; the kingdom of Heaven is theirs" (Matt. 5:3), this beatitude was modeled for him by his mother's life. Mary lived with Jesus and Joseph the life of the beatitudes. They were poor in spirit together and rich in their praise of God.

Mary teaches us how to pray and praise. Our very first step in prayer, our first response to God's choice of us through our creation and redemption, should be based on Mary's response: "My soul magnifies the Lord." As our souls magnify the Lord, we will begin to see, in the literal meaning of the word "magnify," the way of the Lord much more clearly. The small print, as it were, of God's plan for our life will be magnified, enlarged.

Mary's confidence in life is based not on her inner strength, not even on her Immaculate Conception, but on God's fatherly regard. "He has looked on me." God's loving gaze is on each of us. Mary teaches us how to acknowledge and respond to that fatherly interest: "My soul magnifies, my spirit rejoices." Mary teaches us how to become comfortable with our own lowliness and how to accept with confidence what God is asking of us: "He who is mighty has done great things for me." Whatever God is asking of me he himself will do in me.

Pope Paul VI pointed out that "as early as the fourth century St. Ambrose, speaking to the people, expressed the hope that each of them would have the spirit of Mary in order to glorify God: 'May the heart of Mary be in each Christian to proclaim the greatness of the Lord; may her spirit be in everyone to exult God'" (*To Honor Mary* 21). If we begin the new millennium with Mary's heart and spirit, we will learn how to praise God, how to live in the Lord's presence rejoicing in our weakness and how to acknowledge with gratitude the great things that God is doing in our lives.

ॐ

The Spirituality of Mercy

A particular cause for Mary's joy is the mercy of God now incarnate in her womb. She sings: "His mercy is from age to age to those who fear him." This proclamation of the mercy of God is the keynote of the whole song. The very name *Jesus* that she will give to her child is the proof of God's mercy. Jesus means "the one who saves." As the angel said to Joseph, "You must name him Jesus, because he is the one who is to save his people from their sins" (Matt. 1:21). Mary rejoices in God her savior and she rejoices too that the salvation she has received is available to all. Most of all God's mercy is an offer to the humble and the poor. And, as Mary will repeat, "God remembers his mercy." Mary is the prophet of the gospel of the mercy of God.

Our generation needs to be reminded of this abiding reality of the transforming presence of God's mercy. As Pope John Paul II said,

> We have every right to believe that our generation too was included in the words of the Mother of God when she glorified that mercy shared in "from generation to generation" by those who allow themselves to be guided by the fear of God. The words of Mary's *Magnificat* have a prophetic content that concerns not only the past of Israel but also the whole future of the People of God on earth. (*On the Mercy of God* 10)

God's mercy will triumph over all the greed, selfishness, and sinfulness that seem to hold sway in the world. In the darkest moment, when all seems lost either through our own sins or the sins of others, the voice of Mary is heard: "His mercy is from age to age." Mary's word on God's mercy is God's word to us. Because his mercy is from age to age, Mary encourages us never to despair. No matter what the situation, no matter how dark the night, the light and the salvation of our God are at hand. True devotion to Mary is always characterized by a joyful acceptance of her gospel proclamation of the mercy of God. Remembering Mary, without accepting her proclamation of God's mercy, would be a false devotion. God's mercy is with us now. As our generation becomes the first generation of the third millennium to call Mary blessed, she will teach us how to proclaim the mercy of God. We have to be missionaries of the mercy of God in the third millennium.

The first missionaries to Africa began their work of evangelization with an act of consecration, of entrustment to Our Lady. Pope John Paul II referred to this when he spoke in Zaire in 1980:

> Allow me . . . in this year in which you are giving thanks to God for the centenary of the evangelization and the baptism

of your country, to refer to the tradition that we find at the beginning of this century, at the beginning of evangelization in the land of Africa. The missionaries who came to proclaim the Gospel *began their missionary service with an act of consecration to the mother of Christ.*[8]

Embarking on such a wonderful missionary endeavor as the evangelization of the great continent of Africa, those missionaries felt the need of Mary's presence and her continual help. They needed the help and support and protection of the prophet of God's mercy. Cardinal Jean Daniélou explained the connection between Mary and missionary work well when he wrote:

The mystery of the Blessed Virgin lies in the fact that she was in the world before Jesus. This brings us to the specifically missionary aspect of the Marian mystery. Among pagan people the Church does not exist. Hence before pagan nations are converted to Christ, before a local Church becomes visible and established among them, there is a mysterious sense in which Mary is among them preparing for and prefiguring the Church. Her presence is a kind of foreshadowing of what the Church herself will be.[9]

Pope John Paul II makes this view his own when he writes that Mary's "faith precedes the apostolic witness of the Church" (*Redemptoris mater* 27). Before Jesus was born, Mary believed; before there was a church of Christ, Mary was the first and perfect believer in the person of Christ. It is this faith of Mary that missionaries need and to which they are calling people. This is how Pope John Paul concluded his homily on the centenary of the evangelization of Zaire:

Today, a hundred years have passed since these beginnings. At the moment when the Church, in this country of Zaire, thanks God in the Holy Trinity for the waters of baptism that gave salvation to so many of its sons and daughters, permit me, O Mother of Christ and Mother of the Church, permit me Pope John Paul II . . . to recall and at the same time renew this missionary consecration which took place in this land at the beginning of its evangelization.

To consecrate itself to Christ through you!

To consecrate itself to you for Christ.

Permit me also, O Mother of divine grace, while expressing my thanks for all the light that the Church has received and for all the fruit she has yielded in this country of Zaire in the course of this century *to entrust this Church to you again, to place it in your hands again for the years and the centuries to come, to the end of time!*[10]

Mary at the millennium teaches us how to proclaim the mercy of God, but to courageously engage in this proclamation, we have to entrust ourselves, our work, our mission and our message to the Mother of God.

ﻣ

The Spirituality of Liberation

Mary is not just the singer of God's goodness and mercy. She is also the prophet of his justice. God knows what is going on in the world. He made us all equal. He knows that through sin and oppression many of his children have been subjected to the yoke of slavery or exclusion. Those whom God honors have been dishonored; those whom God blesses with the gift of the earth have been impoverished by greed and the lust for money and power. Mary was very aware of the recurring theme in Scripture: "God hears the cry of the poor." She made those sentiments an integral part of her own song of praise and thanks. She proclaimed:

He has used the power of his arm,
  he has routed the arrogant of heart.
He has pulled down princes from their thrones
  and raised high the lowly.
He has filled the starving with good things,
  sent the rich away empty. (Luke 1:51–53)

Having proclaimed God's mercy for those who fear him, Mary now turns to how God deals with the proud. The proud are those who do not fear the Lord. They do not live or feel or act like the poor or the "God fearers." They consider themselves superior, especially to the poor and humble whom Mary represents. Their arrogance and self-centeredness may come from their wealth, their social position or their power. They are presented as the oppressors of the poor. "The proud are the archetypes of sinners: the impious, the evil doers, the unjust, the boastful, scornful of all and humiliating everyone, insatiable in their thirst for power and possessions, oppressors, the violent."[11]

The proud are the enemies of God. And just as God dealt with his enemies in the past, with Pharaoh, Holofernes, Senna-cherib, and the many other oppressors, so God will deal with all the proud. Mary proclaims that God's justice will prevail. Some-times the image we have formed for ourselves of Mary, the gentle maiden, bears little resemblance to the Mary who sings, "My spirit rejoices because he has put down the mighty from their thrones." The kingdom that Mary's Son announces cannot be entered by the proud: "unless you become like little children you cannot enter the kingdom of God." Instead of finding a place in the kingdom, the proud will be "sent away empty."

The Scriptures are full of warnings for the proud. James sums up this when he writes "God opposes the proud but accords his favor to the humble" (Jas. 4:6). The humble, like Mary, are radi-cally dependent on God; they live the glory of God; they are always ready "to hear the word of God and do it." The proud are the opposite. Closed in on themselves, they seek their own glory and find their own security in their wealth or power.

Mary sings about how God has "routed the proud," how he has "pulled down princes from their thrones." But everything seemed to be the same. The proud were still in their places; the wealthy still became wealthier; the unjust rulers still oppressed the poor and the humble. So what did Mary mean? Is her song about a utopian future, a dream world, or is it about a reality? How can she say that God has "pulled down the mighty from their thrones" while the mighty still reign in this world? Elizabeth said that Mary is blessed because "she believed that the promises made to her by the Lord will be fulfilled." Elizabeth would have understood exactly what her young cousin was singing about. Victory is with the Lord, and the Lord is present with and in Mary.

With the coming of the Lord into this world, the order of justice is restored. This restoration is not yet visible on the historical plane, on the level of day-to-day experience. It is present on the eschatological plane, on the level where God himself judges all things, restores all things, and makes all things new. With the eye of faith, in the power of the Spirit, Mary sees God accomplishing all these things through Jesus her Son and Savior. The proud, the mighty, the arrogant carry on doing what they are doing. They will even torture and crucify her Son. But Mary's faith is invincible. She has seen the victory of God. Like the old man Simeon, she can say "my eyes have seen the salvation which you have made ready in the sight of the nations" (Luke 2:30).

Living the spirituality of the Magnificat, seeing the victory of God over the proud, Mary can face all the challenges and the tribulations of her life. God has definitively intervened in human affairs; salvation is here; victory is here. Hence Mary can shout out her victory: "He has pulled down the mighty from their thrones." Living the spirituality of the Magnificat enables each of us to face the uncertainties and tribulations of our life with serenity. As Scripture says, "Only faith can guarantee the blessings that we hope for, or prove the existence of the realities that are unseen" (Heb. 11:1). Mary did not see with her physical eye the overthrow of the mighty. But she saw it with her eye of faith. And she knew that what she saw in faith was more real and more lasting than the passing things of this world. Mary, we can say, sang her Magnificat not just when things were going well but when things were hard and when all seemed lost. Her pain and desolation, her bitter sorrow at seeing how the proud and the mighty killed her Son did not blind her to what she saw in faith, namely, the victory of God, the salvation brought by Jesus. Our pains and desolations should not blind us either to the victory of God in Christ. The Magnificat can be our prayer not just in times of joy and success but also in times of sorrow and failure. True Marian devotion leads us on the path of rejoicing in God's victory even in the face of rejection and death. Authentic Marian devotion, whatever form it takes, will always be imbued with the spirituality of the Magnificat, always full of Mary's spirit of gentleness and strength, confidence and courage, humility and faith-inspired assurance. Mary's confidence in God's promise was amply rewarded when she saw her Son rise from the dead and take his place at the Father's side in glory. The angel had foretold: "The Lord God will give him the throne of his ancestor David; he will rule over the House of Jacob forever and his reign will have no end" (Luke 1:34). Through her faith and her experience of God's ways, Mary knew how to wait on the Lord. This is the lesson she wishes to teaches us.

The Magnificat is not simply a hymn of thanksgiving for the grace God has given to Mary; it is more like a Manifesto of Salvation, a proclamation of the fidelity of God to his promises and the definitive inauguration of God's kingdom. Because the Magnificat is God's word, declaring what God is doing now, in our "today" of salvation, it can be read and received in every age, in every culture, and in every political and social situation. It speaks as clearly to the commuter in New York as it does to the peasant in medieval Europe or the Bedouin in sixth-century Palestine. In our own time it is Mary's proclamation of God's victorious justice, his reversal of the things and values of this world, which has been rediscovered in a new way. Many women and men struggling in situations of grave injustice recognize in Mary's voice the voice of the poor and the oppressed. And Mary's voice calls them not to resignation but to evangelical combat. Evil must be resisted; injustice must be rectified; inequalities must be equalized. Many Christian men and women find in Mary's song inspiration for their struggle, hope for their deliverance, and joy at the certainty of God's victory. Pope Paul VI, in a magnificent passage that should be much better known in the church, wrote:

> The reading of the divine Scriptures, carried out under the guidance of the Holy Spirit, and with the discoveries of the human sciences and the different situations in the world today being taken into account, will help us to see how Mary can be considered a mirror of the expectations of the men and women of our time. Thus, the modern woman, anxious to participate with decision-making power in the affairs of the community,

will contemplate with intimate joy Mary who, taken into dialogue with God, gives her active and responsible consent, not
to the solution of a contingent problem, but to that "event of
world importance," as the Incarnation of the Word has been
rightly called. The modern woman will appreciate that Mary's
choice of the state of virginity, which in God's plan prepared
her for the mystery of the Incarnation, was not a rejection of
any of the values of the married state but a courageous choice
which she made in order to consecrate herself totally to the
love of God. The modern woman will note with pleasant sur-
prise that Mary of Nazareth, while completely devoted to the
will of God, was far from being a timidly submissive woman or
one whose piety was repellent to others; on the contrary, she
was a woman who did not hesitate to proclaim that God vindi-
cates the humble and the oppressed, and removes the powerful
people of this world from their privileged positions (cf. Lk
1:51–53). The modern woman will recognize in Mary, who
"stands out among the poor and the humble of the Lord," a
woman of strength, who experienced poverty and suffering,
flight and exile (cf. Mt 2:13–23). These are the situations which
cannot escape the attention of those who wish to support, with
the Gospel spirit, the liberating energies of man and of society.
And Mary will appear not as a mother exclusively concerned
with her own divine Son but rather as a woman whose action
helped to strengthen the apostolic community's faith in Christ
(cf. Jn 2:1–12) and whose maternal role was extended and
became universal on Calvary. (*To Honor Mary* 37)

In the justified struggles for human liberation we must retain
within ourselves that spirit of Mary and say, "He looked upon his
lowly servant." Without this strong sense that we belong to God,
a revolution will only succeed in replacing one tyrant with
another. It has been rightly pointed out that if the revolution suc-
ceeds in installing the poor Lazarus in the chair of Dives and
Lazarus forgets that he is the servant of God, there will be no
change. As we begin our journey in the third millennium, we will
need the prophetic spirit of Mary to encourage us to demand justice for the poor, liberation for the oppressed, equality for all the

children of God. Imitating Mary, the first and perfect disciple, will lead us to conform joyfully to the will of God and courageously confront what is not God's will for our church and our society. Far from being timid and submissive in the face of injustice Mary is courageous and prophetic. The bishops of South America wrote:

> In the Magnificat Mary presents herself as the model for all those described by Pope John Paul II: "Those who do not passively accept the adverse circumstances of personal and social life and who are not victims of alienation, as the expression goes today, but who instead join with her in proclaiming that God is the 'avenger of the lowly' and will, if need be, depose the mighty from their thrones."[12]

Mary calls us in our time to look to God for justice. Her spirituality today will inspire saints and martyrs in the cause of human dignity. Those who are engaged in a struggle for justice, human rights, and human dignity will find in Mary's Magnificat a source of inner strength and spiritual purity. As Catharina Halkes says, "We too see our lives and faith as a pendulum between *'fiat'* and 'Magnificat,' between receptivity and praise of God, from which prophetic and creative activity emerge."[13] Women especially should find in Mary a spiritual resource for their struggle in what is still a very masculine church and society. The full implications of what Pope John Paul says may take years to unfold: "The figure of Mary of Nazareth sheds light on *womanhood as such* by the very fact that God, in the sublime event of the Incarnation of his Son, entrusted himself to the ministry, the free and active ministry of a woman" (*Redemptoris mater* 46). Many women in the church today don't feel trusted. Church teaching and discipline with regard to the priesthood have left some women feeling rejected. This is not the place to discuss this acute problem. But it is the place to point out that Pope John Paul's theology of God the Father entrusting his Son "to the free and active ministry of a woman" is a good starting point for a deeper, a truly Marian dialogue on the role of women in the ministry of the church.

&a

The Spirituality of the Promise

He has come to the help of Israel his servant,
   mindful of his mercy
—according to the promise he made to our ancestors—
of his mercy to Abraham
   and to his descendants forever. (Luke 1:54)

Mary rejoices and exults in God not just because of the great things he has done in her, nor because of the great mercy he has shown to the poor, but because "he has come to the help of Israel his servant, mindful of his mercy." Mary speaks as a child of her people, as the Daughter of Israel. In Israel's name she gives thanks to God for remembering his mercy. It is an extraordinary moment of fulfillment. God had promised Abraham that through his seed all mankind would be blessed. Mary, a daughter of Abraham, carries within her womb the one in whom this promise is totally fulfilled. Jesus, as St. Paul says, is "God's 'Yes' to all the promises" (2 Cor. 1:20). He is the Amen (Rev. 3:14). Mary is proclaiming that the covenant which God had made with Abraham and through him with all "sons of Abraham's race and all you Godfearers" (Acts 13:26) has been fulfilled. Mary's Magnificat is the song of the fulfillment of all the promises God has made. She sings with great love: "My spirit rejoices in God my Savior . . . because he has come to the help of Israel his servant."

God does not break his word. His faithfulness to Abraham, Isaac, and Jacob, and David his servant, will be everlasting. Hence the promise:

But you, O Israel, my servant
Jacob, whom I have chosen,
You descendants of Abraham, my friend,
I took you from the ends of the earth
from its farthest corners I called you,
I said "You are my servant."
I have chosen you and not rejected you.

> So do not fear, I am with you;
> do not be dismayed, for I am your God. (Isa. 41:8–9)

God's promise "I am with you" was now fulfilled in Mary's womb in a way surpassing all expectation. God indeed had become Emmanuel, God-with-us. Mary's song, therefore, was her people's welcome to Jesus. Before he was born, the Israel of faith welcomed him and praised God for him through the mouth of his mother. The Israel of faith became the church of Christ. We can, therefore, say that before he was born, the church welcomed him through the mouth of his mother. Mary, the Daughter of Israel, the first daughter of the church, sings and exults in her spirit as the old covenant becomes subsumed and fulfilled in the new. The promises made to Abraham "our father in faith" are fulfilled in Jesus, who is par excellence a son of Abraham (Matt. 1:1). Mary rejoices because God has remembered his mercy.

ૐ

Conclusion

Mary at the beginning of the third millennium still accompanies the church on her pilgrimage of faith and is having a profound influence on the church. Her "Magnificat spirituality" is becoming more and more the spirituality of the church. The great renewal movements in the church have come under the direction and inspiration of her presence. In our renewed liturgy and through the charismatic renewal, we have been recalled to the prayer of praise: we understand and feel in a new way Mary's exultation, "My soul magnifies and my spirit exults." Mary teaches us how to praise. She is singing, as it were, the church into the new millennium. Those who see themselves as the "children of the promise," those to whom God says "you are my servant," will join in Mary's song. We will learn from Mary how to praise God not just with our voices but with our souls and our spirits. We will say with new commitment, "Bless Yahweh, my soul from the depths of my being, his holy name" (Ps. 103:1).

The Mother of Christ and the Church is setting the keynote for the strong movement of worldwide evangelization in the church. She is proclaiming God's mercy: "His mercy is from age to age." Her prophetic proclamation of the mercy of God is being absorbed today in a new way by the preachers of the gospel. The laity especially, the new evangelists of the third millennium, are learning from Mary how to proclaim the gospel of God's mercy throughout the world. If Mary is not with us we will forget God's mercy. "Mary must be on all the ways of the Church's daily life" (John Paul II, *Redeemer of Man* 22). Wherever we go, no matter what situation we find ourselves in, Mary teaches us to say with confidence that "his mercy is from age to age." That is the gospel. To proclaim the mercy of God is the essence of evangelization. Mary, as Pope Paul VI said, is "the star of evangelization" (*To Honor Mary* 22).

In the long struggle for justice and human rights in both society and the church, Mary's prophetic words are being heard afresh with a new vigor: "He puts down the mighty from their thrones and sends the rich away empty." Injustice will not have the last word. God has the last word and that last word has already been spoken. Mary saw in faith the triumph of justice and the reign of her Son. She shares with us her faith vision of the reign of her Son at the heart of our world. Even though injustice still seems to be in place, the reality is that already the true justice of God is in our midst. God has, in the words of Pope John Paul II, "entrusted his Son to the ministry, the free and active ministry of a woman." Mary, risen and glorified in body and soul, is present in the church and with us as our Mother. We can get to know and love her better; we can open the home of our hearts and make a place for Mary our mother; we can allow her song, her spirituality, to become our own song and our own spirituality; we can, above all, imitate God the Father and entrust ourselves completely to Mary. Then our devotion to Mary will be truly based on God's word and we will begin to live deeply and joyfully by the last word, the very last word that Jesus spoke to the disciple on earth: She is your mother.

Notes

Chapter 1
Mary: The First and Perfect Disciple

1. Rosemary Radford Ruether, *Mary: The Feminine Face of the Church* (London: SCM, 1979), 35.

2. Raymond E. Brown et al., *Mary in the New Testament* (Philadelphia: Fortress Press, 1978), 55 n. 96.

3. Denis McBride, *Mark* (Dublin, 1996), 18.

4. George T. Montague, *Mark: Good News for Hard Times* (Ann Arbor, Mich.: Servant Books, 1981), 9.

5. Brown, *Mary in the New Testament,* 54.

6. Walter Brennan, *The Sacred Memory of Mary* (New York: Paulist, 1988), 25.

7. Bertrand Buby, *Mary of Galilee* (New York: Alba House, 1994), 1:62.

8. Brown, *Mary in the New Testament,* 170.

9. Ignace de la Potterie, *Mary in the Mystery of the Covenant* (New York: Alba House, 1992), 18.

10. John McHugh, *The Mother of Jesus in the New Testament* (London: Darton, Longman & Todd, 1975), 65.

11. De la Potterie, *Mary in the Mystery of the Covenant,* 35.

12. Gilberte Baril, *The Feminine Face of the People of God* (London: St. Paul, 1991), 112.

13. Brown, *Mary in the New Testament,* 157.

14. Raymond E. Brown, *The Birth of the Messiah* (London: Geoffrey Chapman, 1993), 464.

15. John Paul II, *Mother of the Church,* ed. Seamus Byrne (Dublin: Mercier, 1987), 115.

16. Brown, *Mary in the New Testament,* 162.

17. E. Schillebeeckx and C. Halkes, *Mary, Yesterday, Today and Tomorrow* (London: SCM, 1993), 68.

Chapter 2
Mary the Mother of the Disciple

1. Ignace de la Potterie, *Mary in the Mystery of the Covenant* (New York: Alba House, 1992), 180.

2. Joseph ,Grassi, *Mary: Mother and Disciple* (Wilmington, Del.: Michael Glazier, 1988), 76.

3. Ibid., 98.

4. Raymond E. Brown, *The Gospel According to John,* Anchor Bible 29 (Garden City, N.Y.: Doubleday, 1966), 1:98.

5. Ibid., 99.

6. De la Potterie, *Mary in the Mystery of the Covenant,* 180.

7. Megan McKenna, *Mary: Shadow of Grace* (London: Darton, Longman & Todd, 1995), 105.

8. Brown, *John,* 1:99.

9. De la Potterie, *Mystery of the Covenant,* 202.

10. St. Bernard, cited by de la Potterie, *Mary in the Mystery of the Covenant,* 200.

11. Kathleen Coyle, *Mary in the Christian Tradition from a Contemporary Perspective* (Leominster: Gracewing House, 1993), 18.

12. De la Potterie, *Mary in the Mystery of the Covenant,* 218.

13. John McHugh, *The Mother of Jesus in the New Testament* (London: Darton, Longman & Todd, 1975), 378.

14. Quoted in de la Potterie, *Mary in the Mystery of the Covenant,* 219.

15. Max Thurian, *Mary, Mother of the Lord, Figure of the Church,* trans. Neville B. Cryer (London: Faith Press, 1963), 163.

Chapter 3
Mary in the Early Church

1. Kathleen Coyle, *Mary in the Christian Tradition from a Contemporary Perspective* (Leominster: Gracewing House, 1993), 18.

2. Bertrand Buby, *Mary of Galilee* (New York: Alba House, 1994), 3:33.

Chapter 4
Mary in the Doctrine of the Church

1. Leonardo Boff, *The Maternal Face of God: The Feminine and Its Religious Expressions* (San Francisco: Harper & Row, 1987), 154.

2. Quoted in I. de la Potterie, *Mary in the Mystery of the Covenant* (New York: Alba House, 1992), 153.

3. St Ignatius, *Ancient Christian Writers* (London: Geoffrey Chapman, 1946), 1:67.

4. Raymond E. Brown, *The Virginal Conception and Bodily Resurrection of Jesus* (London: Geoffrey Chapman, 1974), 21.

5. Ivone Gebara and Maria Clara Bingemer, *Mary, Mother of God, Mother of the Poor* (New York: Burns & Oates, 1989), 106.

6. Jacques Bur, *How to Understand the Virgin Mary* (London: SCM, 1994), 26.

7. Ibid.

8. British Methodist/Roman Catholic Committee, *Mary, Mother of the Lord: Sign of Grace, Faith and Holiness: Towards a Shared Understanding* (London: CTS, 1995), 28.

9. Bur, *How to Understand the Virgin Mary,* 44.

10. Ibid., 44.

11. Gebara and Bingemer, *Mary, Mother of God,* 109.

12. Bur, *How to Understand the Virgin Mary,* 49.

13. Kathleen Coyle, *Mary in the Christian Tradition* (Leominster: Gracewing House, 1993), 36.

14. John Macquarrie, *Mary for All Christians* (London: Harper Collins, 1993), 38.

15. John de Satge, *Mary and the Christian Gospel* (London: SPCK, 1976), 74.

16. Michael O'Carroll, *Theotokos* (Wilmington, Del.: Michael Glazier, 1982), 56.

17. Bur, *How to Understand the Virgin Mary,* 87.

18. Ibid.

Chapter 5
Devotion to Mary

1. *L'Osservatore Romano,* English Weekly Edition, 11 May 1983.

2. John McHugh, *The Mother of Jesus in the New Testament* (London: Darton, Longman & Todd, 1975), 71.

3. Kallistos Ware, "The Mother of God in Orthodox Theology and Devotion," in *Mary's Place in Christian Dialogue,* ed. A. Stacpoole (London, 1986), 180.

4. Ibid.

5. Ibid.

6. Basilea Schlink, *Mary, Mother of the Lord* (London: Marshall Pickering, 1986), 118.

7. *The One Mediator, the Saints and Mary,* ed. H. George Anderson (Minneapolis: Augsburg, 1992), 123.

8. Ibid., 126.

9. Edward Yarnold, S.J., *One in Christ* (Bedford, 1989), 70.

10. J. Neville Ward, *Five for Sorrow Ten for Joy* (London, 1971), ix.

11. Quoted in Jacques Bur, *How to Understand the Virgin Mary* (London: SCM, 1994), 55.

Chapter 6
, Mary in the Public Worship of the Church

1. A. Agnus, "Our Lady in Early Liturgy," *Marian Studies* 19 (1968): 30.

2. Pope John Paul II, *Crossing the Threshold of Hope* (London, 1994), 213.

3. Cardinal Leo Suenens, *The Way Supplement* 45 (June 1982): 9.

4. Tina Beattie, *Rediscovering Mary* (Tunbridge Wells: Burns & Oates, 1995), 42.

5. Joseph Paredes, *Mary and the Kingdom of God* (Slough: St. Paul Publications, 1991), 90.

6. Karl Rahner, *Mary Mother of the Lord* (London: Catholic Book Club, 1962), 73.

7. Full text in Bertrand Buby, *Mary of Galilee* (New York: Alba House, 1994), 3:37–51.

8. Hans Urs von Balthasar, *Mary for Today* (Slough, England: St. Paul Publications, 1987), 29.

Chapter 7
Mary in Private Devotion

1. Pope John Paul II, Angelus Message, 29 October 1978.

2. Neville Ward, *Five for Sorrow Ten for Joy* (London, 1971), xii.

3. Frederick Jones, *Alphonsus de Liguori: The Saint of Bourbon Naples 1696-1787* (Dublin: Gill & Macmillan, 1992), 274.

4. Ibid., 272.

5. Michael O'Carroll, *Theotokos: A Theological Encyclopedia of the Blessed Virgin Mary* (Wilmington, Del: Michael Glazier, 1982), 250.

6. John Eade, "To Be a Pilgrim," *The Tablet*, 6 August 1988, 995-96.

7. Frederick Jelly, "Discerning the Miraculous: Norms for Judging Apparitions and Private Revelations," *Marian Studies* 44 (1993): 48.

Chapter 8
Mary at the Millennium

1. See especially Isidro Goma Civit, *The Song of Salvation: The Magnificat* (Slough, England: St. Paul, 1986).

2. Martin Luther, *Works* (St. Louis: Concordia, 1955–86), 2:125.

3. E. Schillebéeckx and C. Halkes, *Mary, Yesterday, Today and Tomorrow* (London: SCM, 1993), 68.

4. Luther, *Works,* 2:154.

5. Ibid., 158.

6. Goma Civit, *Song of Salvation,* 50.

7. Ibid., 59.

8. Quoted in Armand Robichaud, "Mary and the Missions Today," *Marian Studies,* 38 (1987): 106.

9. Ibid., 110.

10. Ibid., 106.

11. Goma Civit, *Song of Salvation,* 85.

12. Third General Conference of Latin American Bishops: Puebla, 297.

13. Schillebeeckx and Halkes, *Mary, Yesterday, Today and Tomorrow,* 74.

Index

182